MEDITERRANEAN DIET

COOKBOOK FOR BEGINNERS

365 DAYS OF QUICK & EASY MEDITERRANEAN RECIPES
FOR CLEAN & HEALTHY EATING

D1710643

BY DEBBY HAYES

TABLE OF CONTENTS

INTRODUCTION

Close your eyes, and imagine sitting outside at a well-worn-in wooden table at a quaint restaurant on the Mediterranean coast. Bright blue skies above you, and sparkling water beside you. The warm sun embraces you with gentle rays. Your meal is placed in front of you with a generous smile from the waiter. It smells heavenly. The fish is fresh from the sea, and the brightly colored vegetables were harvested that morning.

You may be sitting at your kitchen table, far away from the Mediterranean, but you can still enjoy the fresh, delicious, simple foods served in countries around the Mediterranean Sea. Using the recipes in this book can take you on a culinary journey to parts of the world you may only dream of visiting.

The benefits of the Mediterranean diet far exceed the taste. Scientists noticed that the people living in countries that border the Mediterranean Sea are healthy, well into old age. They live longer, and their health is better than people living in other parts of the world.

Looking at their lifestyles, and the foods they eat, it became clear that these people are living well. They are active every day, mostly walking or cycling to wherever they need to go. They eat fresh food that is grown locally and cooked simply with healthy olive oil. They enjoy their meals with family and friends, sipping on a glass of red wine. They naturally understand the benefits of moderation.

That is why the Mediterranean Diet has become so popular. Year after year, it is ranked as the best diet overall. It is a down-to-earth diet, with an emphasis on healthy foods and moderation. It is a balanced diet, full of variety, making it both satisfying and nutritionally sound.

As a dietitian, my go-to for counselling my patients are the Mediterranean dietary principles. Whether they are seeking advice for weight loss, heart disease, diabetes or general health and wellbeing, the balance and nutrition provided by the Mediterranean Diet address their concerns.

And it is easy to follow. The only foods you are cutting out are the highly processed ones, full of denatured fats and excess sugars. These are not allowed in any diet. Everything else is accounted for. Unprocessed, slow-release carbohydrates, healthy fats from olive oil, nuts and seeds, lean proteins, and lots and lots of vegetables and fruits.

It is a way of eating that comes naturally to many people. And the ratios of each type of food can be easily adjusted to meet your individual needs. If your body thrives on carbohydrates, you can eat a bit more of those. If you do better with more fat - no problem, simply add in more foods that are rich in healthy fats.

Not only will your taste buds thank you for cooking from these recipes, your entire body will feel healthier and more energized. You, too, can live a healthier, longer life by embracing the lifestyle enjoyed by the people living near the Mediterranean Sea.

THE BLUE ZONES: EATING FOR HEALTH AND LONGEVITY

Many people have a good understanding of heart disease. It is so common that if it doesn't affect you directly, Your genes have a role to play in your health, and how well you age, but your lifestyle influences your genes. This concept has been highlighted by the work of Dan Buettner. He has studied the areas of the world where people live longer, and he wrote the book, "The Blue Zones", to express his findings.

There is nothing magical about the color blue, and your health and longevity. Rather, the name came about because Buettner and his team drew blue circles around the locations when they were identified. The areas they studied included Ikaria in Greece, Loma Linda in California, Sardinia in Italy, Okinawa in Japan, and Nicoya in Costa Rica.

Buettner identified these areas because the people living there have lower rates of chronic diseases, and live well into old age. He wanted to know why. Buettner and his team found some similarities in the lifestyles of the people living in these communities:

- **They eat plenty of vegetables**
- **Legumes, such as beans, lentils, and chickpeas, form the basis for many meals**
- **The diet is rich in whole grains**
- **Nuts provide protein and healthy fats**
- **Fish is eaten in the Blue Zones that are situated near the sea**
- **A calorie restriction is a normal way of life**
- **They practice periodic fasting**
- **Alcohol is enjoyed in moderation**
- **Daily physical activity is a part of everyday life**
- **Sleep is a priority. People in the Blue Zones get enough sleep at night, and take afternoon naps.**
- **Spirituality is important**
- **As well as having a purpose in life**
- **Older people are not separated from their families**
- **They have a strong social network**

Two of the Blue Zones fall within the Mediterranean Sea - Ikaria and Sardinia. The same patterns are found in other communities living near the Mediterranean Sea. With decades of research to back it up, the Mediterranean Diet has become the gold-standard for healthy eating. It promotes a healthy weight, keeps chronic diseases at bay, and helps people live longer.

WHAT IS THE MEDITERRANEAN DIET?

The word "diet" has come to mean "weight loss diet" for many people. It is, in fact, a term that refers to the way you eat. It doesn't matter whether you choose healthy foods that promote health and wellbeing, or if your preference is for ultra-processed, fatty, sugar-filled foods. Either way, your choice of food would be referred to as your diet.

If you apply this way of thinking to the Mediterranean Diet, it is the way people eat in that part of the world. It is not a diet that has been formulated by science for a specific purpose. It is a diet that has evolved over thousands of years to keep people fed and nourished.

It is a diet that is based on fresh local produce, and making the most of simple ingredients when they are at their best. Most meals are plant-centric. Whole grains, legumes, and vegetables are the heroes of your meal. Meat, fish, and chicken play a supporting role, adding protein and flavor to your dishes.

The food is nutritious and satisfying. Enjoying everything in moderation comes naturally, because your body is receiving all the energy and nutrients it needs to function at its best. The Mediterranean way of eating is not restrictive; everything is allowed. It is a diet that encourages you to live your life to the fullest, enjoying every meal, and being able to socialize, guilt-free, with friends and family.

THE HEALTHY MEDITERRANEAN LIFESTYLE

The communities of the Mediterranean have a holistic approach to life. Diet is only a part of the bigger picture.

People have strong social connections, which helps to improve both physical and mental health. It has been shown that being involved in your community, and regularly visiting with friends and family, can increase your longevity by up to 50%. It can also help to keep depression and anxiety at bay, and strengthen your immune system. Sitting down to a leisurely meal with family every day, and sipping a glass of red wine, can do wonders for your overall sense of wellbeing.

Daily physical activity is a built-in feature of the Mediterranean lifestyle. Instead of spending hours in the car, people will walk or cycle to work. They walk down the road to buy the fresh ingredients for their next meal, stopping to chat with friends they meet along the way.

The people living in this region know the benefits of downtime. They take more time off for vacations than the average American. And a midday meal away from their desks, spent with family, is an important part of their day. It is a way of managing stress that comes naturally to them.

THE HEALTH BENEFITS OF THE MEDITERRANEAN DIET

Scientific research continues to show that the Mediterranean diet brings more to the table than delicious food. The people who live in countries bordering the Mediterranean are healthier, and live longer than people living in other parts of the world. The full benefits will be achieved if the holistic lifestyle is embraced, but the diet alone offers many health benefits:

- **Longevity** - The Mediterranean Diet reduces overall mortality by 9%.
- **Reduced risk of cardiovascular disease** - The fiber-rich foods and healthy fats that make up the Mediterranean Diet help to mitigate the risk factors associated with heart disease, including lowering LDL (bad) cholesterol, raising HDL (good) cholesterol, managing weight, and lowering blood pressure.
- **Lower risk of depression** - Unsaturated fatty acids, combined with nutrients from plant foods, help to prevent depression.
- **Can prevent the onset of Type 2 Diabetes** - The risk of developing Type 2 Diabetes, when you eat according to the Mediterranean dietary principles, is reduced by up to 50%.
- **Reduces the risk of some cancers** - Colorectal, lung, liver, and breast cancer rates are significantly lower in countries in the Mediterranean region than they are in other parts of the world. It is interesting to note that when people move to other countries and adopt their eating habits, the incidence of these cancers rises.
- **Improved cognitive function** - Scientific studies have shown that the Mediterranean Diet can improve cognitive function, and reduce the risk of dementia and Alzheimer's disease.

Use our recipes to dish up a plate full of health and wellbeing. Support both your physical and mental health with fresh, wholesome ingredients in the right proportions, with a dash of healthy fats for good measure.

EMBRACE THE PRINCIPLES OF THE MEDITERRANEAN DIET

People living in different regions of the Mediterranean Basin have different styles of eating, and varied food preferences. The fresh ingredients available are not the same from one area to the next, but they share the basic principles of the Mediterranean Diet.

The meals the Mediterranean people eat are mostly plant-based. The ingredients used for creating meals are in-season, fresh, and locally sourced. The focus is on unprocessed foods that includes whole grain cereals, and fresh fruits and vegetables. Olive oil is the main source of added fat, with more healthy fats coming from fish, nuts, and seeds. Dairy is consumed in moderation, with the focus on fermented products, such as cheese and yoghurt. And red meat and red wine are enjoyed only in moderation.

In combination, these dietary guidelines bring to the table all of the best nature has to offer. When we eat according to these principles, our taste buds are satisfied, our bellies are full, and our bodies are well-nourished.

- **Eat more plants**

Vegetables, fruits, legumes, cereals, nuts, and seeds form the basis of the Mediterranean diet. At least three quarters of your plate will be filled with plant-based foods. They are rich in fiber, vitamins, minerals, and phytonutrients, which all have health and disease-prevention benefits.

Fiber helps to prevent constipation. It also slows down the release of sugars into the blood, helping to control blood sugar levels, and prevent the onset of Type 2 Diabetes. Soluble fiber binds to cholesterol, and prevents its absorption into the blood. It therefore helps to lower blood cholesterol levels, and prevent heart disease.

The micronutrients support all biochemical processes in the body. They are involved in the process of extracting energy from the food we eat, boosting the immune system, and controlling inflammation in the body. They also help to lower your blood pressure, and reduce the risk of cancer.

- **Eat what is fresh and in-season**

When you eat fresh, seasonal produce, you are maximizing the nutrition those foods have to offer. The less time between harvesting and eating, the better. The nutritional value of plant foods starts to decline as soon as they are removed from the earth, or the plant on which they grow. It is even better if they come from local sources, and have not had to spend time in storage, or in transit. The more time spent out of the ground or off the plant before being eaten, the more nutrients are lost.

- **Choose whole grains**

Unprocessed and wholegrain carbohydrates provide energy to the body, in the form of starch, vitamins, and minerals, as well as soluble and insoluble fibers. Whole wheat pasta, cous-cous, barley, bulgar, and polenta are commonly used in Mediterranean cuisine. They take a lot longer to be digested than refined carbohydrates. They are released more slowly into the blood, in the form of glucose, resulting in a gentle rise in blood sugar levels, and therefore lower insulin levels. Including whole grains in your diet has been shown to reduce the risk of obesity, heart disease, certain cancers, and Type 2 Diabetes.

- **Enjoy healthy fats**

Monounsaturated fats are found in olives, olive oil, avocado pears, dark, oily fish, and nuts and seeds. They offer protection against heart disease by lowering total- and LDL-cholesterol levels, and increasing HDL-cholesterol levels. They have anti-inflammatory properties, helping to control inflammation in the body, which underlies many health conditions, including obesity, dementia, and arthritis. Most of the fats in a Mediterranean-style diet come from foods that are a rich source of these essential fats.

- **Eat fish twice a week**

When it comes to animal sources of protein, fish is the focus in the Mediterranean Diet. Whether it is dark, oily fish, like tuna, trout, salmon, sardines, or mackerel, or white fish, such as halibut, hake, sole, or whiting, the goal is to include fish in your menu at least twice a week. The dark, oily fish is a particularly good source of omega-3 fatty acids, which help to lower cholesterol levels, and protect the body against inflammation.

- ## Cook vegetarian meals twice a week

Legumes, in the form of beans, lentils, and chickpeas, are frequently used as a plant source of protein. They are extremely versatile. They can be used in pasta dishes, stews, and soups, or pureed to make dips and spreads, such as hummus. They are a source of low GI carbohydrates, protein, and soluble fiber. They are useful for controlling blood sugar levels, and for reducing the risk of colon cancer and cardiovascular disease.

If you enjoy these nutritional powerhouses, you are not limited to including them only twice a week. You can eat them as often as you like. If they are new to you, start experimenting with our tasty, legume-based meals. You can soak them and cook them from scratch, but the tinned options are just as good, and much quicker to prepare. Just remember to rinse them well to remove the salt.

- ## Cheese and yoghurt in moderation

Small portions of cheese and yoghurt are included in the Mediterranean diet. Milk is not routinely consumed in this region, but a small amount of the fermented products is eaten every day. It could be some Greek yoghurt for breakfast, and a small portion of cheese as a snack, or to add flavor to a salad. The fermentation process makes these products more gentle on the digestive system, by reducing the amount of lactose in them. They also provide a source of beneficial bacteria that are good for gut health. A healthy gut has been shown to have health benefits throughout the body. An unhealthy gut has been linked to weight gain/loss, Type 2 Diabetes, heart disease, brain function problems, and depression and anxiety.

- ## Limit red meat

Very little red meat is eaten in the Mediterranean diet. When it is part of a meal, it is only in small amounts. By reducing how much red meat you eat, you reduce the amount of saturated fat in the diet. Saturated fat provides the building blocks for cholesterol. While we need some cholesterol in our blood, to make hormones and other structures in the body, consuming too much has been linked to heart disease.

- ## Enjoy a glass of wine

If you enjoy a glass of wine with your meal - especially red wine - you are more than welcome to continue drinking it. But it is not an essential component of the Mediterranean Diet. You don't have to start drinking if it is not for you. The antioxidants in red wine have been shown to reduce inflammation in the body, and reduce the risk of heart disease.

- ## Moderation is key

Everything is allowed in the Mediterranean Diet, even cake. But only in moderation. The people of this region understand that too much of a good thing is bad for their health. That includes the good foods, too. Eating too many calories causes weight gain and disease, even if those calories come from healthy foods.

THE WONDERFUL ARRAY OF FOODS TO CHOOSE FROM

Foods to focus on	Foods to limit
When you move away from boxed processed foods, and fill your pantry with colorful, fresh ingredients, you are opening up a world of tasty opportunities. Choosing seasonal foods means that your culinary creations change with the seasons, offering you a wide variety of foods and flavors. Choose from: - All fresh vegetables - especially lots of greens and tomatoes - All seasonal fruits - Fresh herbs, for lots of zesty flavor - The best quality, cold-pressed, extra virgin olive oil - Garlic - All nuts and seeds - Greek yoghurt - Cheese - Oily fish, such as salmon, sardines, mackerel, and trout - All legumes	The Mediterranean Diet allows for most foods to be included from time to time. But certain foods should be limited: - All refined carbohydrates, such as white bread, white pasta, foods made with white flour - Red meat - Processed deli meats - Sugary foods, such as sweets, chocolates, and cold drinks - Excessive alcohol - Refined seed oils

A NOTE ON OLIVE OIL

Olive oil is the main source of added fat in the Mediterranean Diet. It is used for cooking food, as a salad dressing, drizzled over roasted vegetables, and used in place of butter on bread. It is a source of unsaturated fats, especially monounsaturated fats. They have been shown to be useful in lowering cholesterol levels, and reducing chronic inflammation. Use the best quality, cold-pressed, extra virgin olive oil you can buy.

THE MEDITERRANEAN DIET FOR HEALTH AND LONGEVITY

The Mediterranean Diet is healthy eating at its best. It provides the ideal balance of unrefined carbohydrates, lean proteins, and healthy fats, combined with nutrient-dense, fresh seasonal produce. Meals cooked according to the Mediterranean Diet principles are full of intense natural flavor.

Our recipes are guided by these principles, so that you can cook great tasting meals for your family and friends. Not only will your food be delicious, but it will be full of healthful ingredients, putting you on the path to good health and longevity.

28 Day Meal Plan

B. Breakfast   **L.** Lunch   **D.** Dinner

DAY 1	DAY 2	DAY 3	DAY 4	DAY 5
B. Honey-Sweetened Greek Yogurt **L.** Pan-Crisped Mushroom Gnocchi Salad **D.** Olive Baked Cod Fillets	**B.** Fruity Breakfast Couscous **L.** Curried Duck & Winter Vegetables **D.** White Bean, Zucchini & Squash Casserole	**B.** Fruity Yogurt-Topped Avocado Salad **L.** Spicy Mackerel & Kelp Bowls **D.** One-Pan Chicken Pecan Bake	**B.** Spanish Style Toasted Tomato Baguettes **L.** Balsamic-Dressed Calamari Salad **D.** Ricotta Salata Pasta	**B.** Swiss Chard Breakfast Pizza **L.** Fresh Mint & Toasted Pita Salad **D.** Greek-Style Pan-Roasted Swordfish

DAY 6	DAY 7	DAY 8	DAY 9	DAY 10
B. Mediterranean Breakfast Panini **L.** Zesty Lettuce Wrapped Chicken Gyros **D.** Two-Way Tilapia Fillets	**B.** Zesty Fruit Parfaits **L.** Mediterranean-Style Tuna Salad **D.** Lemon Simmered Chicken & Artichokes	**B.** Salmon & Swiss Chard Crepes **L.** Yam & Bean Bowls **D.** Very-Berry Sweet Chili Salmon Fillets	**B.** Avocado Topped Curry Shakshuka **L.** Avocado Tossed Shrimp Salad **D.** Italian-Style Slow Cooker Chicken	**B.** Pan-Fried Haloumi & Greens **L.** Turkish-Style Grilled Meatballs **D.** Asian-Style Cod Bake

DAY 11	DAY 12	DAY 13	DAY 14	DAY 15
B. Breakfast Egg & Bean Cups **L.** Choriatiki Salad **D.** Crispy Chicken & Cabbage Noodles	**B.** Breakfast Surf & Turf **L.** Herb-Marinated Chicken & Radish Salad **D.** Herb-Infused Seafood Paella	**B.** Herb Encrusted Italian Omelet **L.** Coconut-Marinated Salmon Bowls **D.** Cauliflower Steaks & Romesco Sauce	**B.** Pumpkin-Spiced Autumn Quinoa **L.** Curried Duck & Winter Vegetables **D.** Cinnamon Glazed Halibut Fillets	**B.** Quick & Easy Ham & Eggs **L.** Curried Chickpea Burgers **D.** Stir-Fried Chicken & Barley

DAY 16	DAY 17	DAY 18	DAY 19	DAY 20
B. Honey-Sweetened Greek Yogurt **L.** Fresh Mint & Toasted Pita Salad **D.** Nutty Butternut Couscous	**B.** Fruity Breakfast Couscous **L.** Zesty Scallops & Pasta **D.** Ouzo & Orange Glazed Duck	**B.** Fruity Yogurt-Topped Avocado Salad **L.** Spicy Yogurt-Marinated Chicken Skewers **D.** Thai-Spiced Crispy Mackerel Fillets	**B.** Spanish Style Toasted Tomato Baguettes **L.** Yam & Bean Bowls **D.** Lemon Simmered Chicken & Artichokes	**B.** Mediterranean Breakfast Panini **L.** Croatian Double-Crusted Vegetable Tart **D.** Greek-Style Pan-Roasted Swordfish

DAY 21	DAY 22	DAY 23	DAY 24	DAY 25
B. Zesty Fruit Parfaits **L.** Pan-Crisped Mushroom Gnocchi Salad **D.** Olive Baked Cod Fillets	**B.** Salmon & Swiss Chard Crepes **L.** Greek-Style Chicken Couscous **D.** One-Pot Curried Halloumi	**B.** Avocado Topped Curry Shakshuka **L.** Mediterranean-Style Tuna Salad **D.** One-Pan Chicken Pecan Bake	**B.** Pan-Fried Haloumi & Greens **L.** Avocado Tossed Shrimp Salad **D.** Italian-Spiced Mushroom Beanballs	**B.** Breakfast Egg & Bean Cups **L.** Yogurt-Topped Squash Fritters **D.** Ground Turkey Mince

DAY 26	DAY 27	DAY 28		
B. Herb Encrusted Italian Omelet **L.** Coconut-Marinated Salmon Bowls **D.** Vegetable & Herb Chicken Cacciatore	**B.** Pumpkin-Spiced Autumn Quinoa **L.** Ground Turkey Patties in Green Sauce **D.** Crispy vegetable Paella	**B.** Quick & Easy Ham & Eggs **L.** Healthy Tuna & Bean Wraps **D.** Traditional Greek Wine Braised Octopus		

BREAKFASTS

HONEY-SWEETENED GREEK YOGURT

COOK TIME: 0 MINS | MAKES: 2-3 SERVINGS

INGREDIENTS:

- 1/3 tsp. pure vanilla essence
- 2 cups plain Greek yogurt
- 1/4 - 1/2 cup raw honey
- 1/3 tsp. ground nutmeg
- 1 cup blueberries

DIRECTIONS:

1. In a medium-sized glass bowl, whisk together the vanilla and yogurt. Gradually whisk in a small amount of honey, tasting the sweetness as you go, and adding the honey to taste, but not exceeding 1/2 a cup. Once the yogurt is sweetened to your liking, whisk in the nutmeg.

2. Scrape the yogurt into serving bowls, and garnish with the blueberries before serving.

Per Serving:
Calories: 295; Total Fat: 11g; Saturated Fat: 5.5 g; Carbohydrates: 55g; Protein: 23g; Sodium: 82mg; Fiber: 2g

FRUITY BREAKFAST COUSCOUS

COOK TIME: 15 MINS | MAKES: 4 SERVINGS

INGREDIENTS:

- 1 cinnamon stick
- 3 cups milk
- 1/4 tsp. Himalayan salt
- 2 tbsp. raw honey (extra for serving)
- 1/4 cup dried raisins
- 1/2 cup dried apricots, chopped
- 1 cup raw whole-wheat couscous
- 4 tsp. melted butter

DIRECTIONS:

1. Place the cinnamon stick, along with the milk, in a medium-sized pot over medium-high heat, and heat to just under a boil. You want the milk to gently simmer, but not boil.

2. Transfer the pot to a wooden chopping board, and gently whisk in the salt, honey, raisins, apricots, and couscous. Place a lid over the pot, and allow the mixture to stand for about 15 minutes, or until the couscous has softened.

3. Divide the couscous between four bowls, and serve topped with 1 teaspoon of butter per bowl, and extra honey if desired.

Per Serving:
Calories: 333; Total Fat: 8g; Saturated Fat: 5g; Carbohydrates: 54g; Protein: 12g; Sodium: 266mg; Fiber: 3g

FRUITY YOGURT-TOPPED AVOCADO SALAD

COOK TIME: 0 MINS | MAKES: 6 SERVINGS

INGREDIENTS:

- 3 medium-sized ripe avocados, peeled and cubed
- 2 tbsp. lemon juice (plus 1 tsp.)
- 1 tsp. finely grated lemon zest
- 2 tbsp. raw honey
- 1/2 cup plain Greek yogurt
- 1 medium-sized firm banana, sliced
- 11 oz. canned mandarin oranges, drained
- 1 cup seedless grapes, halved
- 1 granny smith apple, chopped

DIRECTIONS:

1. Place the cubed avocados in a bowl with 2 tablespoons of lemon juice, and toss to coat.

2. In a separate bowl, whisk together the remaining lemon juice, lemon zest, honey, and yogurt.

3. Add the banana, mandarin oranges, grapes, and apple to the bowl with the avocado, and gently toss to combine.

4. Scoop the salad into bowls, and serve topped with the yogurt.

Per Serving:
Calories: 231; Total Fat: 11g; Saturated Fat: 2g; Carbohydrates: 35g; Protein: 3g; Sodium: 22mg; Fiber: 6g

SPANISH-STYLE TOASTED TOMATO BAGUETTES

COOK TIME: 8 MINS | MAKES: 4 SERVINGS

INGREDIENTS:

- 2 baguettes, halved lengthwise
- 4 tsp. crushed garlic
- 2 ripe heirloom tomatoes, grated
- 2 tbsp. extra-virgin olive oil
- 4 thin slices smoked ham
- Freshly ground black pepper
- 1 tsp. flaky sea salt

DIRECTIONS:

1. Set the oven to preheat to 500°F, with the wire rack in the center of the oven.

2. Arrange the baguette halves on a baking tray with the open sides up, and toast in the oven for 6-8 minutes, or until nicely browned and crispy.

3. When the baguettes are nicely toasted, spread 1 teaspoon of crushed garlic over the face of each baguette. Top the garlic with grated tomato. Spread the tomato out in an even layer, using a butter knife.

4. Sprinkle a small amount of olive oil over the tomatoes. Top each baguette with a slice of ham, and season to taste with black pepper, before seasoning each baguette with the salt. Use about 1/4 teaspoon of salt per baguette.

5. Plate the toasted baguettes, and serve straight away.

Per Serving:
Calories: 267; Total Fat: 15g; Saturated Fat: 4g; Carbohydrates: 15g; Protein: 18g; Sodium: 1,295mg; Fiber: 3g

SWISS CHARD BREAKFAST PIZZA

COOK TIME: 15 MINS | MAKES: 6 SERVINGS

INGREDIENTS:

- 1 thin base, 12-inch, prebaked pizza base
- 3/4 cup reduced fat ricotta cheese
- 1 tsp. sweet smoked paprika (divided)
- 1 tsp. garlic powder
- 1/2 cup sundried tomatoes (not packed in oil)
- 1 cup baby mushrooms, sliced
- 3 cups Swiss chard, roughly chopped
- 2 tbsp. extra-virgin olive oil
- 2 tbsp. balsamic vinegar
- 1/4 tsp. white pepper, divided
- 1/4 tsp. Himalayan salt
- 6 large free-range eggs

DIRECTIONS:

1. Set the oven to preheat to 450°F, with the wire rack in the center of the oven.

2. Place the pizza base on a large baking tray. Use a knife to spread the ricotta cheese over the base in an even layer. Sprinkle 1/2 teaspoon of paprika over the cheese, along with 1 teaspoon of garlic powder.

3. Top the seasoned cheese with sundried tomatoes and sliced mushrooms.

4. Place the Swiss chard in a large bowl, and sprinkle with oil, vinegar, and 1/8 teaspoon each of pepper and salt. Use clean hands to toss and coat the chard in the seasoning for a few minutes, until softened and well coated.

5. Arrange the seasoned chard on top of the pizza. Create a nest in the chard for each individual egg. Carefully crack each egg into a nest, and season with the remaining paprika, pepper, and salt.

6. Bake the pizza in the oven for 12-15 minutes, or until the egg whites are no longer runny, and the yellow is almost set, but not completely.

7. Slice, and serve hot.

Tip: Sun dried tomatoes may need to be softened before use if you are not using the oil-packed kind. Simply soak the tomatoes in boiling water until soft, and drain before use.

Per Serving:
Calories: 299; Total Fat: 13g; Saturated Fat: 4g; Carbohydrates: 31g; Protein: 15g; Sodium: 464mg; Fiber: 5g

MEDITERRANEAN BREAKFAST PANINI

COOK TIME: 0 MINS | MAKES: 4 SERVINGS

INGREDIENTS:

- 1 (12oz.) round panini loaf
- 2 tbsp. extra-virgin olive oil
- 8 large free-range eggs, hard-boiled, and sliced into rounds
- 1/2 cup black olives, pitted and halved
- 2 heirloom tomatoes, thinly sliced into rounds
- 12 large, fresh basil leaves

DIRECTIONS:

1. Slice the panini loaf in half horizontally, and use a basting brush to coat the inside of each slice with 1 tablespoon of olive oil.

2. Begin building the panini by placing a single layer of boiled egg slices on one half of the panini, followed by the olives, tomato rounds, and finally, the basil leaves.

3. Place the remaining panini slice on top. Slice the panini, and serve.

Per Serving:
Calories: 427; Total Fat: 21g; Saturated Fat: 5g; Carbohydrates: 39g; Protein: 23g; Sodium: 674mg; Fiber: 7g

ZESTY FRUIT PARFAITS

COOK TIME: 0 MINS | MAKES: 4 SERVINGS

INGREDIENTS:

- 2 cups reduced-fat plain Greek yogurt
- 1 tsp. pure vanilla essence
- 2 tbsp. chia seeds
- 2 tsp. finely grated lemon zest
- 2 tbsp. fresh lemon juice
- 1/4 cup raw honey
- 1 cup fresh blueberries
- 1 cup fresh strawberries, halved

DIRECTIONS:

1. In a medium-sized bowl, whisk together the yogurt, vanilla, chia seeds, lemon zest, lemon juice, and honey.

2. Divide half of the yogurt mixture between four serving bowls. Followed by 1/2 cup each of blueberries and strawberries. Repeat the process with the remaining yogurt and fruit.

3. Serve immediately.

Per Serving:
Calories: 214g; Total Fat: 4g; Saturated Fat: 2g; Carbohydrates: 33g; Protein: 13g; Sodium: 48mg; Fiber: 5g

SALMON & SWISS CHARD CREPES

COOK TIME: 15 MINS | MAKES: 2 SERVINGS

INGREDIENTS:

- 1 cup fresh Swiss chard, chopped
- 1 tbsp. flax meal
- 1 tbsp. nutritional yeast
- 1/4 tsp. crushed dried thyme
- 1 small bunch fresh parsley, chopped
- Himalayan salt
- Freshly ground black pepper
- 2 large free-range eggs
- 2 tsp. extra-virgin olive oil
- 3 oz. wild smoked salmon
- 1/2 large Hass avocado, sliced
- 2 tbsp. feta, crumbled
- 1 tsp. fresh lemon juice

DIRECTIONS:

1. Combine the Swiss chard, flax meal, nutritional yeast, thyme, and parsley in a blender. Add a pinch of salt and pepper, or more to taste, before pulsing the mixture until the chard is fine. Add the eggs, and pulse until the mixture just comes together.

2. In a large frying pan over medium heat, heat 1 teaspoon of olive oil. When the oil is hot, add half of the chard mixture, and gently move the pan around until the mixture is evenly distributed over the bottom. Fry for about 3 minutes, or until the crepe is no longer jiggly, but not completely firm.

3. Top the crepe with half of the salmon, avocado, and feta. Drizzle the whole crepe with 1 teaspoon lemon juice, while still in the pan. Carefully transfer the crepe to a plate, and keep warm while you repeat the process with the remaining ingredients.

4. Serve the crepes warm, and enjoy.

Per Serving:
Calories: 679; Total Fat: 49.2g; Saturated Fat: 11.6g; Carbohydrates: 6.6g; Protein: 44.4g; Fiber: 12.7g

AVOCADO-TOPPED CURRY SHAKSHUKA

COOK TIME: 15 MINS | MAKES: 4 SERVINGS

INGREDIENTS:

- 4 tbsp. extra-virgin olive oil (divided)
- 1 small zucchini, chopped
- 1 small green bell pepper, sliced
- 1 tsp. crushed garlic
- 1/2 small shallot, chopped
- 1/2 tsp. sweet smoked paprika
- 1/4 tsp. ground cilantro seeds
- 1/2 tsp. ground turmeric
- 1/2 tsp. ground cumin
- 1/2 cup canned tomatoes, whole or chopped
- 3.5 oz. fresh Swiss chard, roughly chopped
- 4 large free-range eggs
- 1/4 cup goat's cheese, grated
- 1 small Hass avocado, sliced
- 2 tsp. fresh lemon juice

DIRECTIONS:

1. Set the oven to preheat to 425°F, with the wire rack in the center of the oven.

2. In a large, oven-safe frying pan, heat 2 tablespoons of olive oil over medium heat. When the oil is nice and hot, fry the zucchini, bell pepper, garlic, and shallots for about 3-4 minutes, or until the shallots are translucent, and the vegetables have softened. Stir in the paprika, cilantro seeds, turmeric, and cumin for 30 seconds, allowing the fragrances to meld. Add the tomatoes and chard to the pan, frying for about 1 minute, or until the chard has reduced.

3. Remove the pan from the heat. Use a wooden spoon or ladle to create pockets in the shakshuka. Carefully crack each egg into its own individual pocket, taking care not to damage the yolks. Bake in the oven for 5-8 minutes, or until the whites are no longer runny, but the yellow is not yet firm.

4. Transfer the pan to a wooden chopping board, and garnish the shakshuka with the goat's cheese and avocado slices. Drizzle with the remaining olive oil and lemon juice. Serve hot, and enjoy.

Per Serving:
Calories: 573; Total Fat: 49.3g; Saturated Fat: 10.7g; Carbohydrates: 9.2g; Protein: 20g; Fiber: 7.9g

PAN-FRIED HALOUMI & GREENS

COOK TIME: 15-20 MINS | MAKES: 4 SERVINGS

INGREDIENTS:

- 4 tbsp. extra-virgin olive oil (divided)
- 2 tsp. fresh rosemary, chopped
- 1 tsp. crushed garlic
- 1 medium zucchini, roughly chopped
- 1 small eggplant, roughly chopped
- 1 tbsp. freshly squeezed lemon juice
- 1 tbsp. fresh oregano, chopped
- 2 tbsp. fresh mint leaves, chopped
- Himalayan salt
- Freshly ground black pepper
- 6 oz. Haloumi cheese, sliced or cut
- 4 large boiled eggs, sliced
- 1/4 cup black olives, pitted and halved

DIRECTIONS:

1. In a large frying pan over medium heat, heat 2 tablespoons of olive oil. When the oil is nice and hot, fry the rosemary and garlic for about 1 minute, or until fragrant. Add the zucchini, eggplant, and lemon juice to the pan, stirring until everything is combined. Turn down the heat to medium-low, and allow the vegetables to cook covered for 10-15 minutes, or until softened, stirring occasionally to prevent burning.

2. Stir in the oregano and mint. Season to taste with salt and pepper, before scraping the vegetables onto a serving platter, and tenting with foil to keep in the heat.

3. Use greaseproof paper to wipe the inside of the pan, removing any excess juices and oil. Return the pan to medium heat, and add 1 tablespoon of olive oil. When the oil is hot, fry the halloumi for about 3 minutes per side, or until the edges are nice and crispy.

4. Serve the fried halloumi on a bed of warm vegetables, topped with sliced eggs, black olives, and 1 tablespoon of the olive oil drizzled over everything.

Per Serving:
Calories: 679; Total Fat: 58g; Saturated Fat: 17.9g; Carbohydrates: 8.6g: Protein: 27.7g; Fiber: 5.2g

BREAKFAST EGG & BEAN CUPS

COOK TIME: 20 MINS | MAKES: 4 SERVINGS

INGREDIENTS:

- 2 tbsp. avocado oil
- 2 tsp. crushed garlic
- 1 small sweet onion, diced
- 1/2 tsp. white pepper
- 1 tsp. Himalayan salt
- 1/4 tsp. red pepper flakes
- 1/4 tsp. ground cumin
- 1/2 tsp. sweet smoked paprika
- 14 oz. canned white beans, rinsed and drained
- 14 oz. canned diced tomatoes
- 1 link spicy chorizo, thinly sliced
- 4 large free-range eggs

DIRECTIONS:

1. Set the oven to preheat to 400°F, with the wire rack in the center of the oven.

2. Heat the oil in a medium-sized pan over medium heat, before adding the garlic and onions. Fry the onions for about 3 minutes, or until they become translucent.

3. Stir in the pepper, salt, red pepper flakes, cumin, paprika, white beans, and tomatoes with the juice from the can. Continuously stir for about 8 minutes, or until the sauce reduces and becomes thicker. Remove the pan from the heat.

4. Arrange four medium or large baking cups, such as ramekins, on a baking tray. Divide the beans and tomato mixture evenly between the cups. Top with the chorizo slices, divided between the four cups.

5. Create a pocket in each cup, and carefully crack each egg into its own pocket. Bake in the oven for 10-12 minutes, or until the egg whites are firm, but the yellow is still soft. Serve hot in the ramekin cups.

Per Serving:
Calories: 605; Total Fat: 23g; Saturated Fat: 7g; Carbohydrates: 66g; Protein: 37g; Sodium: 1,105mg; Fiber: 17g

BREAKFAST SURF & TURF

COOK TIME: 5-10 MINS | MAKES: 2 SERVINGS

INGREDIENTS:

- 3 large free-range eggs
- Yolk of 1 large free-range egg
- 1/4 cup grated parmesan cheese
- 1/4 tsp. ground turmeric
- 2 tbsp. extra-virgin olive oil (divided)
- 1 medium green onion, chopped, and white and green parts separated
- Himalayan salt
- Freshly ground black pepper
- 1/2 cup salmon roe

DIRECTIONS:

1. In a medium-sized glass bowl, whisk together the three whole eggs, the egg yolk, cheese, and turmeric.

2. In a large pan over medium heat, heat 1 tbsp. olive oil, before adding the white parts of the green onion, and frying for about 2-3 minutes.

3. Once the onions are fragrant, carefully pour the egg mixture into the pan. Move the pan around so that the egg is evenly distributed over the bottom. Season to taste with salt and pepper. Using a spatula, gently coax the edges of the egg towards the center of the pan. The uncooked egg will spill over and cook. When the eggs are just about cooked, and almost firm, transfer the pan to a wooden chopping board, and allow the eggs to rest for a few minutes in the pan.

4. Gently stir the remaining olive oil through the eggs. Scrape the eggs onto 2 plates, and top with the salmon roe, and the green parts of the green onion, before serving.

Per Serving:
Calories: 581; Total Fat: 50.5g; Saturated fat: 15.4g; Carbohydrates: 6.1; Protein: 28.7g; Fiber: 0.5g

HERB-ENCRUSTED ITALIAN OMELET

COOK TIME: 15-20 MINS | MAKES: 4 SERVINGS

INGREDIENTS:

- 1 tbsp. extra-virgin olive oil
- 1/4 cup shallots, thinly sliced
- 1 large Yukon gold potato, thinly sliced
- 1/8 tsp. white pepper
- 1/8 tsp. cayenne pepper
- 1/4 tsp. Himalayan salt
- 1/4 tsp. dried thyme, crushed
- 1/4 tsp. dried rosemary, crushed
- 6 large free-range eggs
- 2 tbsp. grated mozzarella cheese

DIRECTIONS:

1. Set the oven broiler to preheat on high, with the wire rack in the center of the oven.

2. In a large, oven-safe frying pan, heat the oil before adding the shallots, and frying for 2-3 minutes, or until the shallots have softened. Use a slotted spoon to transfer the cooked shallots to a separate dish, and tent to keep warm. Place the potato slices in the bottom of the pan in a single layer.

3. Add the pepper, cayenne pepper, salt, thyme, rosemary, and eggs to the bowl of shallots. Lightly whisk until the eggs are light and fluffy. Pour the egg mixture over the potatoes. Cover the pan with tin foil, and bake in the oven for 4-6 minutes, or until the eggs are no longer runny, but not completely set.

4. Remove the pan from the oven, and discard the foil. Sprinkle the cheese over the omelet before returning the pan to the oven, and broiling for 2-5 minutes. The cheese should be lightly toasted, and the eggs completely set.

5. Allow the omelet to rest for about 5 minutes outside the oven, before slicing and serving.

Per Serving:
Calories: 204g; Total Fat: 12g; Saturated Fat: 4g; Carbohydrates: 13g; Protein: 11g; Fiber: 1g

PUMPKIN-SPICED AUTUMN QUINOA

COOK TIME: 30 MINS | MAKES: 4 SERVINGS

INGREDIENTS:

- 1/2 cup quinoa, rinsed
- 3/4 cup steel-cut oats
- 1/4 tsp. kosher salt
- 3 cups water
- 3 tbsp. raw honey
- 1 tsp. pumpkin pie spice
- 3/4 cup canned pumpkin
- 1/3 cup lightly toasted walnuts, roughly chopped
- 1/2 cup dried cranberries
- Almond milk

DIRECTIONS:

1. Bring the quinoa, oats, salt, and water to a boil, in a medium pot over medium heat. Once the mixture is boiling, lower the heat, and simmer with the lid on the pot for 20 minutes, stirring occasionally to prevent burning.

2. Gently stir in the honey, pumpkin spice, and canned pumpkin. Transfer the pot to a wooden chopping board, and allow to stand with the lid on the pot for about 5 minutes, or until all of the liquids are absorbed, and the quinoa and oats have softened.

3. Gently stir in the walnuts and dried cranberries. Serve with a few splashes of almond milk, if desired.

Per Serving:
Calories: 361; Total Fat: 10g; Saturated Fat: 1g; Carbohydrates: 65g; Protein: 9g; Sodium: 155mg; Fiber: 7g

QUICK & EASY HAM & EGGS

COOK TIME: 2 MINS | MAKES: 1 SERVING

INGREDIENTS:

- 1/8 tsp. white pepper
- 1/8 tsp. sweet smoked paprika
- 1 large egg
- Whites of 2 large eggs
- 2 tbsp. mozzarella cheese, grated
- 1 spring onion, chopped
- 1 slice deli ham, chopped
- 2 whole-wheat pita pocket halves

DIRECTIONS:

1. Place the pepper, paprika, egg, and egg whites in a medium-sized glass bowl. Whisk until the eggs are light and fluffy. Add in the cheese, spring onions, and ham, stirring gently to combine.

2. Place the bowl in the microwave for about 1 minute, before stirring and microwaving for an additional 30-60 seconds, or until the eggs are properly cooked.

3. Spoon the cooked eggs and ham into the pita halves, and serve.

Per Serving:
Calories: 323; Total Fat: 10g; Saturated Fat: 4g; Carbohydrates: 334g; Protein: 27g; Sodium: 769mg; Fiber: 5g

SNACKS & APPETIZERS

SAVORY MUSHROOM PANCAKES

COOK TIME: 15-20 MINS | MAKES: 2 SERVINGS

INGREDIENTS:

- 1/2 cup almond milk
- 1/2 cup chickpea flour
- 6 tbsp. extra-virgin olive oil (divided)
- Himalayan salt
- 8 oz. button mushrooms, stems removed
- 3 fresh thyme sprigs
- Freshly ground black pepper
- 1 bunch Swiss chard, ribs removed, finely chopped

DIRECTIONS:

1. In a medium-sized bowl, whisk together the milk, flour, 2 tablespoons of olive oil, and a small pinch of salt, until you have a nearly smooth batter. Set the batter aside to rest for 15 minutes while you prepare the rest of the dish.

2. Heat 1 tablespoon of olive oil in a large skillet over medium heat. When the oil is nice and hot, add the mushrooms, thyme, 1/8 teaspoon of salt, and a pinch of black pepper. Fry the mushrooms for about 5 minutes, or until they darken. Scrape the cooked mushrooms into a bowl, and keep warm.

3. Heat 1 tablespoon of oil in the same skillet, and add the chard, along with another 1/8 teaspoon salt, and an extra pinch of black pepper. Fry the chard for about 5 minutes, or until all the leaves have wilted. Scrape the cooked chard into the same bowl with the mushrooms, and keep warm.

4. Use a crumpled piece of greaseproof paper to clean any excess vegetables and oil from the skillet. Return the skillet to medium heat, and add 1 tablespoon of oil. When the oil is hot, beat the batter once more, to incorporate as much air as possible. Add half of the batter to the hot oil, gently swirling the skillet to coat the bottom. Fry the pancake for 2-3 minutes, before flipping, and frying the other side until lightly browned – about 2-3 minutes. Flip the pancake onto a plate, and repeat the process with the remaining oil and batter.

5. Serve the pancakes warm, and topped with cooked mushrooms and chard.

Per Serving:
Calories: 530; Total Fat: 45g; Carbohydrates: 26g; Protein: 11g; Sodium: 490mg; Fiber: 10g

SPICY HERB & TUNA BOCADILLO

COOK TIME: 20 MINS | MAKES: 4 SERVINGS

INGREDIENTS:

- 3 tbsp. extra-virgin olive oil
- 2 leeks, white and tender green parts only, finely chopped
- 1 medium shallot, finely chopped
- 1/2 tsp. dried marjoram
- 1 tsp. chopped thyme
- 1/2 tsp. kosher salt
- 1/4 tsp. white pepper
- 1 carrot, finely chopped
- 3 tbsp. balsamic vinegar
- 8 oz. canned Spanish tuna in olive oil
- 4 crusty whole-wheat sandwich rolls, split
- 1 large heirloom tomato, finely grated
- 4 piquillo peppers, thinly sliced

DIRECTIONS:

1. In a medium-sized frying pan over medium heat, heat 2 tablespoons of olive oil. When the oil is nice and hot, add the leeks, shallots, marjoram, thyme, salt, and pepper. Fry and toss the vegetables for about 10 minutes, or until the shallots become translucent. Add the carrots and vinegar, tossing for an additional 5 minutes, until most of the juices have cooked away. Scrape the contents of the pan into a bowl, and allow to cool slightly before chilling.

2. When the vegetables are properly chilled, add the tuna, along with the oil, to the bowl, and mix using a fork, until all of the ingredients are properly combined.

3. Use a basting brush to lightly coat the rolls with the remaining tablespoon of oil, before placing them under the broiler for a few minutes, until lightly toasted.

4. Divide the grated tomato between the rolls, and use a butter knife to spread it over the bottom half of each roll.

5. Spoon the tuna mixture onto each roll, and top with the peppers before slicing and serving.

Per Serving:
Calories: 412; Total fat: 23g; Saturated Fat: 3g; Carbohydrates: 26g; Protein: 31g; Sodium: 948mg; Fiber: 3g

YOGURT-TOPPED SQUASH FRITTERS

COOK TIME: 10 MINS | MAKES: 4-6 SERVINGS

INGREDIENTS:

- 6 small yellow squash, grated
- 1 1/4 tsp. Himalayan salt (divided)
- 1/2 lemon, juiced
- 2 tsp. sweet smoked paprika
- 1 cup plain Greek yogurt
- 1/4 tsp. white pepper
- 1/2 cup all-purpose flour
- 3 large free-range eggs, beaten
- 4 spring onions, thinly sliced
- 1/4 cup fresh parsley, finely chopped
- 4 oz. feta cheese, crumbled
- olive oil for frying

DIRECTIONS:

1. Toss the grated squash in a large bowl with 1 teaspoon of salt. Transfer to a colander set over the sink, and allow to drain for at least 20 minutes. Use the back of a wooden spoon or ladle to gently press any excess water from the vegetables, before transferring them back to a bowl.

2. In a small glass bowl, whisk together the lemon juice, paprika, yogurt, and 1/4 teaspoon of salt. Set aside.

3. Add the pepper, flour, eggs, spring onions, parsley, and crumbled feta to the bowl with the squash, gently stirring to combine.

4. In a large frying pan over medium-high heat, heat 1/2-inch of oil. Test the oil by inserting the tip of a toothpick – the oil is ready when the toothpick immediately begins to sizzle. Use a ladle to carefully drop the batter into the hot oil – about 4-5 fritters at a time. Lightly flatten the fritters with a spatula, and fry for 2 minutes. Flip, and fry the other side for an additional 2 minutes, or until both sides are lightly browned.

5. Transfer the cooked fritters to a serving platter, and keep warm.

6. Serve the fritters warm, topped with the yogurt dressing.

Per Serving:
Calories: 237; Total Fat: 14g; Saturated fat: 2g; Carbohydrates: 18g; Protein: 11g; Sodium: 655mg; Fiber: 3g

SPICY MEDITERRANEAN TAPENADE

COOK TIME: 0 MINS | MAKES: 16 SERVINGS

INGREDIENTS:

- 1/4 tsp. dried thyme
- 3 tsp. crushed garlic
- 1 tbsp. capers, drained
- 1 tbsp. fresh parsley, chopped
- 2 tbsp. extra-virgin olive oil
- 2 tbsp. freshly squeezed lime juice
- 1/4 cup chopped poblano peppers
- 1/2 cup black olives, pitted
- 1/2 cup red bell peppers, chopped
- 16 thin slices of French baguette, lightly toasted

DIRECTIONS:

1. Place the thyme, garlic, capers, parsley, olive oil, lime juice, poblano peppers, olives, and bell peppers in a food processor, and pulse on high until you have a smooth paste.

2. Spread about 1 tablespoon of the tapenade over each slice of lightly toasted baguette, and serve.

Per Serving:
Calories: 63; Total Fat: 3g; Saturated Fat: 0g; Carbohydrates: 7g; Protein: 1g; Sodium: 183mg; Fiber: 0g

RAINBOW TROUT HERB PATE

COOK TIME: 0 MINS | MAKES: 16 SERVINGS

INGREDIENTS:

- 2 tsp. fresh parsley, finely chopped
- 1/8 tsp. white pepper
- 1 tbsp. lime juice
- 1 tbsp. horseradish sauce
- 1/2 cup half-and-half cream
- 3 oz. reduced-fat cream cheese
- 1 lb. flaked smoked rainbow trout
- 16 cucumber slices
- 16 assorted crackers

DIRECTIONS:

1. In a food processor, pulse the parsley, pepper, lime juice, horseradish sauce, cream, cream cheese, and trout on high, until you have a smooth paste.

2. Arrange the 16 crackers on a serving platter, and top each with a thin slice of cucumber. Place about 1 teaspoon of pate onto each cucumber slice, and serve.

Per Serving:
Calories: 55; Total Fat: 3g; Saturated Fat: 1g; Carbohydrates: 1g; Protein: 5g; Sodium: 174g; Fiber: 0g

MEDITERRANEAN DEVILED EGGS

COOK TIME: 0 MINS | MAKES: 12 SERVINGS

INGREDIENTS:

- 6 large free-range eggs, hard-boiled
- 1/8 tsp. white pepper
- 1/8 tsp. kosher salt
- 1/2 tsp. freshly squeezed lemon juice
- 1/8 tsp. sweet smoked paprika
- 1/2 tsp. finely grated lemon zest
- 1 tsp. dried oregano
- 2 tbsp. feta cheese, crumbled
- 3 tbsp. reduced-fat mayonnaise
- 12 black olives, pitted

DIRECTIONS:

1. Carefully slice the boiled eggs in half, and use a teaspoon to remove the yolks. Place the whites on a serving platter. Transfer 4 yolks to a medium-sized bowl, and discard the rest, or freeze for another use.

2. Add the pepper, salt, lemon juice, paprika, zest, oregano, cheese, and mayonnaise to the bowl with the yolks. Use a fork to beat and mash the mixture, until you have a smooth paste.

3. Spoon or pipe the yolk mixture into the egg whites, and garnish with the olives before serving.

Per Serving: Calories: 42; Total Fat: 3g; Saturated Fat: 1g; Carbohydrates: 1g; Protein: 3g; Sodium: 96mg; Fiber: 0g

CHEESY, ALMOND-CRUSTED CHARD PIE

COOK TIME: 1 HOUR | MAKES: 16 SERVINGS

INGREDIENTS:

- 3 tbsp. cool water
- 1 tbsp. flaxseed meal (plus 2 tsp.)
- Freshly ground black pepper
- 1/8 tsp. kosher salt (plus 1/4 tsp.)
- 1/2 tsp. dried oregano
- 1 cup almond flour
- 1 tbsp. avocado oil
- 1 tbsp. extra-virgin olive oil

- 2 tsp. crushed garlic
- 1/2 medium shallot, finely chopped
- 10 oz. Swiss chard
- 1/2 tsp. dried oregano
- 5 oz. soft goat cheese, grated
- 2 large free-range eggs
- 1/4 cup almond slivers

DIRECTIONS:

1. Set the oven to preheat to 350°F, with the wire rack in the center of the oven. Spray a large casserole dish with baking spray, and set aside.

2. Place the water in a medium-sized bowl, along with the flaxseed meal, and gently combine. Lightly beat in a pinch of freshly ground black pepper, along with the salt, oregano, and almond flour. Add the oil, and mix until the ingredients come together to form a dough. Use your hands to gather the dough together, and press it tightly into the prepared casserole dish. Press up the sides, as well, to form a rim. Bake the crust in the oven for about 18 minutes, or until golden brown.

3. Meanwhile, heat the olive oil in a large pot over medium-low heat. When the oil is hot, fry the garlic and shallots for about 5 minutes, or until the shallots are tender and translucent. Stir in the chard, and fry for about 2 minutes, until the chard has reduced in size.

4. Transfer the pot to a wooden chopping board, and stir in the remaining 1/4 teaspoon of salt, a large pinch of pepper, oregano, cheese, and eggs.

5. Scoop the filling into the prebaked crust, and sprinkle with the almond slivers before returning the pie to the oven, and baking for an additional 28 minutes, or until the filling is firm, and the almonds are lightly toasted.

6. Slice, and serve hot, or chill for a tasty snack.

Per Serving:
Calories: 113; Total Fat: 9g; Carbohydrates: 3g; Protein: 5g; Sodium: 122g; Fiber: 2g

CHEESY PICKLED BEET BITES

COOK TIME: 12 MINS | MAKES: 72 SERVINGS

INGREDIENTS:

- 72 frozen, miniature phyllo tart shells
- 1 jar pickled whole beets, drained and chopped
- 1 tsp. finely grated orange zest
- 2 tsp. fresh rosemary, chopped
- 1/4 tsp. oregano
- 1/4 tsp. freshly ground black pepper
- 1 tbsp. extra-virgin olive oil
- 2 cups fresh arugula, torn
- 3/4 cup crumbled feta cheese

DIRECTIONS:

1. Prebake the tart shells in an oven at moderate heat for about 12 minutes, or until the shells are all nicely browned. Allow them to cool on a wire rack.

2. Drain the beets through a colander set over the sink. Use paper towels to pat the beets dry before transferring them to a large mixing bowl. Add the orange zest, rosemary, oregano, pepper, and olive oil, stirring to combine.

3. Divide the arugula between the baked shells, and spoon the pickled beets into each. Top with the feta, and serve.

Per Serving:
Calories: 31; Total Fat: 1g; Saturated Fat: 0g; Carbohydrates: 3g; Protein: 1g; Sodium: 33mg; Fiber: 0g

OLIVE-STUFFED CHICKEN BREASTS

COOK TIME: 8-10 MINS | MAKES: 4 SERVINGS

INGREDIENTS:

- 2 tbsp. balsamic vinegar
- 1 tbsp. extra-virgin olive oil
- 4 tsp. crushed garlic
- 1/4 cup roasted sweet red peppers, drained
- 4 green olives, pitted
- 4 Spanish olives, pitted
- 4 black olives
- 4 oil-packed sun-dried tomatoes
- 4 boneless chicken breasts, skins removed
- Grated Parmesan cheese, for garnishing

DIRECTIONS:

1. In a blender, pulse the vinegar, oil, garlic, sweet peppers, olives, and tomatoes on medium, until you have a lumpy paste.

2. Slice the chicken breasts open, taking care not to cut all the way through. Divide the olive paste between the breasts and use a spoon to fill each one.

3. Spear the breasts closed with toothpicks to ensure that none of the filling escapes.

4. Place the stuffed breasts on a lightly coated rack, and broil in the oven on high for 8-10 minutes, or until the chicken is properly cooked. Keep an eye on the chicken to ensure it doesn't burn.

5. Remove the toothpicks and serve hot, garnished with the cheese.

Per Serving:
Calories: 264; Total Fat: 11g; Saturated Fat: 2g; Carbohydrates: 5g; Protein: 35g; Sodium: 367mg; Fiber: 1g

SPICY CRAB BITES

COOK TIME: 12 MINS | MAKES: 30 SERVINGS

INGREDIENTS:

- 30 miniature, frozen phyllo tart shells
- 1/2 tsp. seafood seasoning
- 1/2 cup reduced-fat spreadable garden vegetable cream cheese
- 1/2 tsp. freshly ground black pepper
- 1/3 tsp. cayenne pepper
- 1/3 cup lump crab meat, drained
- 5 tbsp. hot sauce

DIRECTIONS:

1. Cook the miniature tart shells according to package instructions, and allow to cool completely on a wire rack.

2. In a medium-sized mixing bowl, whisk together the seafood seasoning, cream cheese, black pepper, and cayenne pepper. Gently stir in the crab meat, until all of the ingredients are properly combined.

3. Spoon the mixture into the cooled phyllo shells, and top with a few splashes of hot sauce before serving.

Per Serving:
Calories: 34; Total Fat: 2g; Saturated Fat: 0g; Carbohydrates: 3g; Protein: 1g; Sodium: 103mg; Fiber: 0g

ZESTY CUCUMBER & YOGURT DIP

COOK TIME: 0 MINS | MAKES: 4-6 SERVINGS

INGREDIENTS:

- 1 medium English cucumber
- 1/2 small fennel bulb
- Freshly ground black pepper
- Himalayan salt
- 2 tbsp. fresh dill, chopped
- 1 tsp. crushed garlic
- 1 tsp. finely grated lemon zest
- 2 tbsp. freshly squeezed lemon juice
- 5 tbsp. avocado oil (divided)
- 2 cups plain Greek yogurt

DIRECTIONS:

1. Grate the cucumber into a large bowl, and use the back of a wooden spoon to press out and drain any excess fluids.

2. Place the fennel bulb in a food processor, and pulse on high until finely chopped. Scrape the chopped fennel bulb into the bowl with the cucumber.

3. Season the cucumber and chopped fennel with a large pinch each of salt and pepper. Stir in the dill, garlic, zest, lemon juice, 3 tablespoons of oil, and the yogurt, until all of the ingredients are properly combined. Drizzle with the remaining oil, and serve.

Tip: Leftover dip can be stored in the fridge, using an airtight container, for no more than 5 days.

Per Serving:
Calories: 223; Total Fat: 19.7g; Saturated Fat: 7g; Carbohydrates: 5.7g; Protein: 6.4g; Fiber: 0.7g

SCRUMPTIOUS CURRY ROASTED CHICKPEAS

COOK TIME: 40 MINS | MAKES: 4 SERVINGS

INGREDIENTS:

- 15 oz. canned chickpeas, drained and rinsed
- 2 tbsp. avocado oil
- 1 tsp. ground turmeric powder
- 1/4 tsp. Himalayan salt
- White pepper
- 1 tsp. ground sumac

DIRECTIONS:

1. Cover a large baking tray with greaseproof paper, and set the oven to preheat to 350°F, with the wire rack in the center of the oven.

2. Place a clean kitchen towel on the counter, and pour the drained chickpeas over the towel in a single layer. Cover the chickpeas with a second clean towel. Roll the chickpeas gently with your hands, so that the towels dry the chickpeas properly. This process is crucial to ensure the chickpeas roast properly, and reach the desired level of crispiness.

3. Transfer the dried chickpeas to a medium-sized bowl, and sprinkle with the oil, turmeric, salt, a large pinch of pepper, and sumac. Toss until all of the chickpeas are evenly coated in the spices.

4. Spread the chickpeas out in an even layer across the prepared baking tray. Bake in the oven for 40 minutes, or until all of the chickpeas are a crispy golden brown.

5. Remove the tray from the oven, and allow the chickpeas to dry out before sealing in a container, or serving immediately.

Per Serving:
Calories: 120; Total Fat: 9g; Carbohydrates: 9g; Protein: 3g; Sodium: 189mg; Fiber: 3g

ROAST BEEF & ASPARAGUS BUNDLES

COOK TIME: 3 MINS | MAKES: 16 SERVINGS

INGREDIENTS:

16 fresh asparagus spears, trimmed
- 1/8 tsp. ground cumin
- 1 tsp. lemon juice
- 1 tsp. French mustard
- 1 tsp. crushed garlic
- 1/3 cup mayonnaise
- 8 thin slices deli roast beef, cut in half lengthwise
- 3 different colored medium sweet peppers, thinly sliced
- 16 whole chives
- Freshly ground black pepper

DIRECTIONS:

1. Bring a small pot of water to a rolling boil. When the water is boiling, add the asparagus spears, and boil for no more than 3 minutes. Strain the asparagus spears immediately after boiling, and place them in a bowl of ice water. Strain again, and pat completely dry.

2. In a small glass bowl, whisk together the cumin, lemon juice, mustard, garlic, and mayonnaise.

3. Lay the roast beef slices out over a clean work surface. Top each slice of roast beef with 1 teaspoon of the mayonnaise mixture, using the back of the teaspoon to spread it out. Place 1 asparagus spear on each beef slice, and top with slices of each color sweet pepper. Sprinkle with black pepper before rolling up the bundles, and securing them with the chive strands.

4. Serve immediately.

Per Serving:
Calories: 52; Total Fat: 4g; Saturated Fat: 1g; Carbohydrates: 2g; Protein: 2g; Sodium: 74mg; Fiber: 1g

FIERY HOMEMADE TOMATO-TOPPED FRIES

COOK TIME: 1 HOUR | MAKES: 6 SERVINGS

INGREDIENTS:

- 4 large Yukon gold potatoes, sliced into thin fries
- 1/4 cup extra-virgin olive oil (plus 1 tbsp.)
- Kosher salt
- Freshly ground black pepper
- 1 serrano chili, seeded and chopped
- 1 tsp. hot smoked paprika
- 1 tsp. cayenne pepper
- 1 1/2 tsp. red wine
- 1/2 cup crushed tomatoes

DIRECTIONS:

1. Set the oven to preheat to 425°F, with the wire rack in the center of the oven.

2. In a large bowl, toss the fries with 1/4 cup of olive oil, and a large pinch each of salt and pepper, until properly coated. Spread the fries out over a baking tray, and bake in the oven for 50-60 minutes, or until the fries are soft on the inside, and crispy on the outside.

3. While the fries are roasting in the oven, place the chili, paprika, cayenne pepper, red wine, tomatoes, 1/2 teaspoon salt, 1/4 teaspoon pepper, and 1 tablespoon olive oil in a food processor, and pulse on high until you have a lump-free sauce.

4. Serve the fries hot, with the sauce spooned over the top, or as an optional dip on the side.

Per Serving:
Calories: 201; Total Fat: 11g; Saturated Fat: 2g; Carbohydrates: 25g; Protein: 3g; Sodium: 243mg; Fiber: 4g

ZESTY WHITE WINE MARINATED OLIVES

COOK TIME: 0 MINS | MAKES: 4 SERVINGS

INGREDIENTS:

- 1/2 tsp. cayenne pepper
- 4 tsp. crushed garlic
- 3 tbsp. no-salt-added seasoning blend
- 1/4 cup sunflower oil
- 1/2 cup white wine
- 3 tbsp. orange juice
- 3 tbsp. lime juice
- 3 tbsp. lemon juice
- 2 tsp. finely grated orange zest
- 2 tsp. finely grated lime zest
- 2 tsp. finely grated lemon zest
- 4 cups mixed pitted olives

DIRECTIONS:

1. In a large bowl, whisk together the cayenne pepper, garlic, seasoning blend, sunflower oil, and wine. Whisk in the orange juice, lime juice, lemon juice, orange zest, lime zest, and lemon zest.

2. Gently stir in the olives. Cover the bowl, and chill for a minimum of 4 hours before serving.

Per 1\4 cup Serving:
Calories: 74; Total Fat: 7g; Saturated Fat: 1g; Carbohydrates: 3g; Protein: 0g; Sodium: 248mg; Fiber: 1g

SALADS & SIDES

MEDITERRANEAN-STYLE TUNA SALAD

COOK TIME: 0 MINS | MAKES: 4 SERVINGS

INGREDIENTS:

- 1 tsp. Himalayan salt
- 3 tbsp. white wine vinegar
- 1/4 cup extra-virgin olive oil
- 1 tsp. crushed garlic
- 1 medium red bell pepper, seeded and diced
- 1 cup pitted green olives
- 6 oz. canned tuna in olive oil, well-drained
- 1 bag mixed salad greens

DIRECTIONS:

1. Place the salt, vinegar, and oil in a large mixing bowl. Whisk until properly combined.

2. Gently stir in the garlic, bell peppers, and olives. Add the drained tuna, and stir until all of the ingredients are properly combined. Seal the bowl, and chill for a minimum of 1 hour.

3. Serve the chilled tuna mixture on a bed of mixed salad greens.

Per Serving:
Calories: 343; Total Fat: 28g; Saturated Fat: 4g; Carbohydrates: 6g; Protein: 21g; Sodium: 1,217mg; Fiber: 2g

BALSAMIC-DRESSED CALAMARI SALAD

COOK TIME: 5-10 MINS | MAKES: 4 SERVINGS

INGREDIENTS:

- 1/4 cup balsamic vinegar
- 1 tsp. raw honey
- 1 lb. calamari, thawed and patted dry
- Extra-virgin olive oil
- Pinch cayenne pepper
- Himalayan salt
- 1 tsp. crushed garlic

- 2 tsp. freshly squeezed lemon juice
- 1 small zucchini, thinly sliced
- 8 cups baby arugula
- 2 oz. parmesan cheese, finely grated
- 8 oil-packed sundried tomatoes
- Freshly ground black pepper

DIRECTIONS:

1. In a small pot over medium heat, bring the balsamic vinegar to a gentle simmer. Continue to simmer the vinegar for about 4 minutes, or until about half of it has evaporated. Transfer the pot to a wooden chopping board, and gently whisk in the honey.

2. Prepare the calamari by slicing each tentacle into 1/4-inch rings, taking extra care to slice the large tentacles down the middle. This will ensure that the calamari does not cook unevenly.

3. In a large skillet over medium-high heat, heat the olive oil before adding the calamari, cayenne pepper, 1/4 teaspoon salt, and crushed garlic. Fry the calamari rings for about 4 minutes, or until all of the rings are completely solid. Use tongs to transfer the cooked calamari to a separate bowl, and keep warm.

4. With the skillet still over medium-high heat, stir the sauce for about 3 minutes, until it is thick enough to coat the back of a teaspoon. Spoon the thickened sauce over the calamari, and drizzle with lemon juice.

5. Arrange the zucchini slices on a serving platter, and drizzle with 1 tablespoon of olive oil, and 1/8 teaspoon of salt. Arrange the baby arugula on top of the zucchini slices, and drizzle with the balsamic reduction. Top with the parmesan cheese in an even layer. Decorate the outer edges of the salad plate with the sundried tomatoes.

6. Place the cooked calamari in the center of the salad plate, and garnish with freshly ground black pepper before serving.

Per Serving:
Calories: 284; Total Fat: 18g; Carbohydrates: 11g; Protein: 25g; Sodium: 703mg; Fiber: 3g

PUMPKIN-TOPPED AUTUMN RICE

COOK TIME: 35-40 MINS | MAKES: 2 SERVINGS

INGREDIENTS:

- 1 small pie pumpkin
- 1 tbsp. extra-virgin olive oil
- 1 cup water
- 1/2 cup raw brown basmati rice
- 1/8 tsp. ground cardamom
- 1/8 tsp. ground cinnamon
- 1/4 tsp. turmeric powder
- 1/4 tsp. kosher salt
- 2 tbsp. raisins
- 3 dried apricots, chopped
- 1/4 cup lightly toasted pecans, chopped
- 1/8 tsp. ground cumin

DIRECTIONS:

1. Set the oven to preheat to 400°F, with the wire rack in the center of the oven. Peel and gut the pumpkin, before slicing it into 6 wedges. Discard the innards of the pumpkin. Place the pumpkin wedges in a large mixing bowl, and toss to coat with the olive oil. Fan the coated pumpkin wedges out on a clean baking sheet, and bake in the oven for 35-40 minutes, or until the wedges are fork-tender.

2. While the pumpkin bakes in the oven, bring the water and rice to a rolling boil. Once the rice is boiling, lower the heat, and simmer covered for 20-25 minutes, or until the rice is properly cooked. When the rice is properly cooked, stir in the cardamom, cinnamon, turmeric, salt, raisins, apricots, and pecans.

3. Scoop the rice onto a serving platter, and top with the roasted pumpkin wedges. Sprinkle the cumin over everything, and serve hot.

Per Serving:
Calories: 389; Total fat: 15g; Saturated Fat: 2g; Carbohydrates: 62g; Protein: 7g; Sodium: 309mg; Fiber: 5g

CRISPY BALSAMIC RAISIN CAULIFLOWER

COOK TIME: 55 MINS | MAKES: 4 SERVINGS

INGREDIENTS:

- 2 lb. cauliflower florets
- 6 tbsp. extra-virgin olive oil (divided)
- 1 tsp. kosher salt
- 1/2 tsp. freshly ground black pepper
- 3 tsp. crushed garlic
- 2 tbsp. salt-packed capers, rinsed and patted dry
- 3/4 cup fresh whole-wheat bread crumbs
- 1 tsp. anchovy paste
- 1/2 cup chicken stock
- 1 tbsp. balsamic vinegar
- 1/3 cup golden raisins
- 1 tbsp. fresh parsley, chopped

DIRECTIONS:

1. Set the oven to preheat to 425°F, with the wire rack in the center of the oven.

2. Place the cauliflower florets, 3 tablespoons of oil, salt, and pepper in a large mixing bowl. Toss until all of the florets are evenly coated. Arrange the coated florets on a clean baking tray, and bake for about 45 minutes, turning every few minutes, or until the florets are tender, and nicely browned.

3. Meanwhile, heat the remaining olive oil in a large skillet over medium-low heat. When the oil is nice and hot, fry the garlic for about 5 minutes. Stir in the capers, and fry for an additional 3 minutes. Stir in the bread-crumbs, and fry for a few more minutes, stirring throughout, until the crumbs are nicely toasted. Use a slotted spoon to scoop the fried bread crumbs into a clean bowl.

4. Turn up the heat to medium-high, and whisk the anchovy paste and chicken broth into the same skillet used to fry the breadcrumbs. When the stock begins to boil, whisk in the balsamic vinegar and raisins. Continue to cook for an additional 5 minutes, or until the stock has reduced, and the raisins are swollen.

5. Place the cooked cauliflower florets in a large mixing bowl, and toss with the bread crumbs and raisins. Transfer the mixture to a serving dish, and garnish with the parsley before serving.

Per Serving:
Calories: 366; Total Fat: 24g; Saturated Fat: 3g; Carbohydrates: 37g; Protein: 9g; Sodium: 1,102mg; Fiber: 7g

ITALIAN-STYLE OVEN BREAD

COOK TIME: 30-35 MINS | MAKES: 15 SERVINGS

INGREDIENTS:

- 1/4 cup ground chia seeds
- 1/4 cup ground psyllium powder
- 1/2 cup coconut flour
- 1/2 packed cup flax meal
- 1/2 tsp. baking soda
- 1/2 tsp. white pepper
- 1/2 tsp. kosher salt

- 1/2 cup extra-virgin olive oil
- 2 tsp. crushed garlic
- 1 tbsp. crushed rosemary
- 1 tbsp. crushed oregano
- Whites of 8 large eggs
- 1 tsp. white wine vinegar
- 1 cup lukewarm water

DIRECTIONS:

1. Set the oven to preheat to 285°F, with the wire rack in the center of the oven. Line a large baking sheet with tin foil.

2. In a large bowl, whisk together the chia seeds, psyllium powder, coconut flour, flax meal, baking soda, white pepper, and salt. Set aside.

3. In a small glass bowl, whisk together the olive oil, garlic, rosemary, and oregano. Set aside.

4. In a third clean bowl, whisk the egg whites until they form soft peaks, drizzling the vinegar in gradually as you whisk, to help maintain the peaks.

5. Using a stand mixer, add the lukewarm water to the flour, and work as you gradually drizzle half of the oil mixture into the bowl. As soon as the oil is incorporated, gradually add half of the beaten egg whites. Add the remaining egg whites while the mixer is running, until all of the ingredients come together to form a dough.

6. Transfer the dough to the prepared baking sheet, and use your hands to press the dough out onto the sheet. Gently press the dough down with your fingers, creating tiny pockets as you go. Take the remaining olive oil mixture, and use a basting brush to coat the top of the dough. Bake in the oven for 30-35 minutes, or until the bread is a crispy, golden brown.

7. Transfer the cooked bread to a wire rack, and let stand for 5 minutes before slicing into 15 squares, and serving.

Tip: The baked bread can be kept on the counter for up to 3 days, or frozen in an airtight container for no more than 3 months.

Per Serving:
Calories: 128; Total Fat: 10.6g; Saturated Fat: 1.8g; Carbohydrates: 1.2g; Protein: 4.1g; Fiber: 4.5g

MEDITERRANEAN-STYLE MASHED POTATOES

COOK TIME: 20 MINS | MAKES: 4 SERVINGS

INGREDIENTS:

- 2 lbs. russet potatoes, peeled and cubed (1-inch cubes)
- 1 1/2 tsp. kosher salt (divided)
- 2 spring onions, thinly sliced
- 2 tsp. extra-virgin olive oil
- 1/2 cup full cream milk (more if needed)
- 1/2 cup plain Greek yogurt
- 1 tbsp. fresh dill, chopped

DIRECTIONS:

1. Fill a large pot with water to cover the potatoes, and bring to a rolling boil, along with 1 teaspoon of salt. Boil the potatoes for about 15-20 minutes, or until all the potatoes are softened through. Strain the potatoes through a colander set over the sink.

2. Transfer the cooked potatoes to a large mixing bowl, and mash along with the spring onions, olive oil, milk, yogurt, and the remaining 1/2 teaspoon of salt. Add more milk if needed to reach the desired consistency.

3. Spoon into a serving dish, and garnish with the dill before serving.

Per Serving:
Calories: 224; Total Fat: 5g; Saturated Fat: 2g; Carbohydrates: 40g; Protein: 6g; Sodium: 922mg; Fiber: 6g

FRESH MINT & TOASTED PITA SALAD

COOK TIME: 0 MINS | MAKES: 4 SERVINGS

INGREDIENTS:

- 1/4 tsp. freshly ground black pepper
- 1/2 tsp. ground sumac (extra for garnish)
- 1 tsp. Himalayan salt
- 1 tsp. crushed garlic
- 1/2 cup extra-virgin olive oil
- 1/2 cup freshly squeezed lemon juice
- 2 whole-wheat pita bread rounds, toasted, and broken into bite-sized pieces
- 1 bunch spring onions, thinly sliced
- 1 small green bell pepper, diced
- 1/4 cup fresh mint leaves, chopped
- 1/2 cup fresh parsley, chopped
- 2 heirloom tomatoes, diced
- 2 small English cucumbers, diced
- 2 cups romaine lettuce, shredded

DIRECTIONS:

1. In a small glass bowl, whisk together the pepper, sumac, salt, garlic, olive oil, and lemon juice. Set aside.

2. In a large mixing bowl, toss together the toasted pita bites, spring onions, bell pepper, mint, parsley, tomatoes, cucumbers, and shredded lettuce. Drizzle the with the olive oil dressing, and serve immediately, garnished with the extra ground sumac.

Per Serving:
Calories: 359; Total Fat: 27g; Saturated Fat: 4g; Carbohydrates: 29g; Protein: 6g; Sodium: 777mg; Fiber: 6g

CHORIATIKI SALAD

COOK TIME: 0 MINS | MAKES: 4 SERVINGS

INGREDIENTS:

- 1/4 cup capers
- 16 black olives, pitted
- 1 small red onion, sliced
- 1 medium green bell pepper, sliced
- 1 large English cucumber, diced
- 4-5 heirloom tomatoes, chopped
- 7 oz. whole feta wheels (2 wheels)
- 1 tsp. dried oregano
- 1/2 cup extra-virgin olive oil
- Freshly ground black pepper
- Himalayan salt

DIRECTIONS:

1. In a large serving bowl, toss together the capers, olives, onions, bell pepper, cucumber, and tomatoes. Crumble 1 of the feta wheels into the bowl, and toss along with half of the oregano, and half of the olive oil.

2. Place the remaining whole feta wheel on top of the salad, and sprinkle with the remaining oregano and olive oil. Season the salad to taste with pepper and salt before serving. The salad can also be chilled for no more than 1 day, but is best served fresh.

Per Serving:
Calories: 443; Total Fat: 41.3g; Saturated Fat: 12.6g; Carbohydrates: 8g; Protein: 9.3g; Fiber: 3.3g

ZESTY VINAIGRETTE POTATO SALAD

COOK TIME: 20 MINS | MAKES: 12 SERVINGS

INGREDIENTS:

- 3 lbs. red potatoes, cubed
- 1/4 tsp. freshly ground black pepper
- 1 1/2 tsp. Himalayan salt
- 2 tbsp. balsamic vinegar
- 2 tbsp. freshly squeezed lemon juice
- 1/3 cup extra-virgin olive oil
- 1/2 tsp. dried oregano
- 1 tsp. crushed garlic
- 2 tbsp. fresh parsley, finely chopped
- 1/3 cup red onion, chopped
- 1/2 cup Greek olives, pitted and chopped
- 1/2 cup parmesan cheese, grated

DIRECTIONS:

1. In a large pot over medium-high heat, cover the potatoes with water, and bring to a rolling boil. When the water is boiling, lower the heat, and boil for 10-15 minutes, or until the potatoes are fork-tender. Drain the cooked potatoes in a colander set over the sink.

2. In a small glass bowl, whisk together the pepper, salt, vinegar, lemon juice, and olive oil, until all of the ingredients are properly combined. Add the oregano, garlic, and parsley, and stir to combine.

3. Place the drained potatoes in a large bowl, and toss together with the onions, olives, and dressing. Cover the bowl, and chill for a minimum of two hours.

4. Stir in the cheese right before serving, and enjoy.

Per Serving:
Calories: 168; Total Fat: 9g; Saturated Fat: 2g; Carbohydrates: 20g; Protein: 4g; Sodium: 451mg; Fiber: 2g

NUTTY & DENSE SEED BREAD

COOK TIME: 60 MINS | MAKES: 16 SERVINGS

INGREDIENTS:

- 1 tsp. freshly ground black pepper
- 1 tsp. Himalayan salt
- 1/2 cup pecans, chopped
- 1/2 cup blanched hazelnuts, chopped
- 1/2 cup almond slivers
- 1/4 cup sunflower seeds
- 1/4 cup pumpkin seeds
- 1/2 cup sesame seeds
- 1/2 cup chia seeds
- 1/2 cup flaxseeds
- 4 large free-range eggs
- 1/2 cup sunflower oil

DIRECTIONS:

1. Set the oven to preheat to 285°F, with the wire rack in the center of the oven. Line a bread tin with grease-proof paper, leaving a few inches on each side to use as handles.

2. In a large bowl, stir together the pepper, salt, pecans, hazelnuts, almonds, sunflower seeds, pumpkin seeds, sesame seeds, chia seeds, and flax seeds. Add the eggs and oil, and stir until all of the ingredients are properly combined.

3. Scrape the mixture into the prepared bread tin, and even out using a wooden spoon. Bake for about 1 hour, or until the top of the loaf is nicely browned.

4. Allow the bread to cool slightly for a few minutes in the tin, before transferring to a wire cooling rack. Once the bread is completely cool, slice and serve.

Tip: The bread can be stored on the counter for 3 days, chilled for 10 days, or frozen in an airtight container for no more than 3 months.

Per Serving:
Calories: 290; Total Fat: 26.3g; Saturated Fat: 3.2g; Carbohydrates: 2.5g; Protein: 8.2g; Fiber: 6g

PAN-CRISPED MUSHROOM GNOCCHI SALAD

COOK TIME: 20 MINS | MAKES: 14 SERVINGS

INGREDIENTS:

- 2 tbsp. extra-virgin olive oil (plus 1/3 cup)
- 16 oz. potato gnocchi
- 1/2 lb button mushrooms, sliced
- 3 tsp. freshly squeezed lemon juice
- 1/4 tsp. freshly ground black pepper
- 1/2 tsp. Himalayan salt
- 2 tsp. finely grated lemon zest
- 2 tbsp. capers, drained and chopped
- 1/3 cup fresh parsley, chopped
- 1/2 cup Kalamata olives, pitted and halved
- 5 oz. fresh Swiss chard, chopped
- 15 oz. canned chickpeas, drained and rinsed
- 3 large plum tomatoes, seeded and chopped
- 1/4 cup lightly toasted walnuts, chopped
- 1/2 cup feta, crumbled

DIRECTIONS:

1. Heat one tablespoon of oil in a large frying pan over medium-high heat. When the oil is nice and hot, fry the gnocchi for 6-8 minutes, or until golden brown. Scrape the cooked gnocchi into a large mixing bowl, and set aside.

2. Add 1 tablespoon of oil to the same frying pan, and heat. When the oil is nice and hot, fry the mushrooms for about 8 minutes, until they darken in color and release their juices. Scrape the cooked mushrooms into the bowl with the gnocchi.

3. Pour 1/3 cup of oil and 3 tablespoons of lemon juice into the bowl, and gently stir to combine.

4. Add the pepper, salt, lemon zest, capers, parsley, olives, chard, chickpeas, and tomatoes to the bowl, stirring gently to combine.

5. Sprinkle the gnocchi with the walnuts and cheese, and serve immediately.

Per Serving:
Calories: 204; Total Fat: 12g; Saturated Fat: 2g; Carbohydrates: 21g; Protein: 5g; Sodium: 425mg; Fiber: 3g

MEDITERRANEAN-STYLE STEAMED LEEKS

COOK TIME: 8-10 MINS | MAKES: 6 SERVINGS

INGREDIENTS:

- 6 medium leeks, halved lengthwise, and cleaned
- 1/2 tsp. white pepper
- 1/2 tsp. finely grated orange zest
- 1 tsp. extra-virgin olive oil
- 1 tsp. red wine vinegar
- 1 tsp. capers, drained
- 2 tbsp. Kalamata olives, pitted and sliced
- 2 tbsp. fresh parsley, chopped
- 1 small navel orange, peeled, sectioned, and chopped
- 1 large heirloom tomato, chopped
- crumbled feta cheese for topping

DIRECTIONS:

1. Bring a large pot of water to a rolling boil over high heat. When the water is boiling, place a steamer basket or colander over the pot. The water should not be touching the bottom of the basket or colander. Lower the heat to maintain a low boil. Place the leeks in the basket or colander, and seal with the basket lid, or a fitted pot lid, to keep in the steam. Steam the leeks for 8-10 minutes, or just until softened through.

2. While the leeks are steaming, place the pepper, orange zest, oil, vinegar, capers, olives, parsley, orange, and tomato in a mixing bowl, and gently stir until all of the ingredients are properly combined.

3. When the leeks have softened, carefully arrange them on a serving plate, and spoon the contents of the mixing bowl over all of the leeks. Top with the cheese, and serve.

Per Serving:
Calories: 83; Total fat: 2g; Saturated Fat: 0g; Carbohydrates: 16g; Protein: 2g; Sodium: 77mg; Fiber: 3g

LEMON & MINT-TOPPED GARDEN SALAD

COOK TIME: 20 MINS | MAKES: 4 SERVINGS

INGREDIENTS:

- 1/8 tsp. Himalayan salt (extra if needed)
- 1 tsp. fresh mint, chopped
- 2 tbsp. extra-virgin olive oil
- 1 small lemon, juiced
- 1/2 medium English cucumber, thinly sliced
- 1 heirloom tomato, roughly chopped
- 4-5 cups mixed salad greens, shredded
- White pepper

DIRECTIONS:

1. In a small glass bowl, whisk together the salt, mint, olive oil, and lemon juice. Set aside.

2. Place the cucumber, tomato, and salad greens in a bowl. Season to taste with extra salt and pepper, if desired, and toss to combine. Drizzle with the lemon and mint mixture before serving.

Tip: Any extra lemon mixture may be refrigerated, and reserved for other dishes.

Per Serving:
Calories: 80; Total Fat: 7g; Carbohydrates: 2g; Protein: 1g; Sodium: 80mg; Fiber: 2g

CREAMY & CRUNCHY CUCUMBER SALSA

COOK TIME: 0 MINS | MAKES: 4 SERVINGS

INGREDIENTS:

- 1 tsp. crushed garlic
- 4 1/2 tsp. fresh coriander leaves, chopped
- 1 jalapeno pepper, seeded and chopped
- 2 tbsp. fresh flat-leaf parsley, chopped
- 1/4 cup shallots, chopped
- 1/2 cup heirloom tomatoes, chopped
- 2 cups cucumber, seeded and chopped
- 1/4 tsp. Himalayan salt
- 1/4 tsp. ground cumin
- 1 1/2 tsp. freshly squeezed lime juice
- 1 1/2 tsp. freshly squeezed lemon juice
- 1/4 cup reduced-fat sour cream
- Baked tortilla chip scoops for serving

DIRECTIONS:

1. Place the garlic, coriander leaves, jalapeno, parsley, shallots, tomatoes, and cucumber in a medium-sized bowl, stirring gently to combine.

2. In a separate bowl, whisk together the salt, cumin, lime juice, lemon juice, and sour cream.

3. Drizzle the sour cream mixture over the salad, and gently toss until all of the ingredients are evenly coated. Serve immediately, with a side of baked tortilla chip scoops.

Tip: Seeded cucumber is key to keeping the crunchiness in this salad. Halving a cucumber and scooping out the seeds with a teaspoon is the easiest way to do the seeding before chopping.

Per Serving:
Calories: 16; Total fat: 1g; Saturated Fat: 0g; Carbohydrates: 2g; Protein: 1g; Sodium: 44mg; Fiber: 0g

SPICY FRIED FAVA BEANS

COOK TIME: 7 MINS | MAKES: 4 SERVINGS

INGREDIENTS:

- 1 1/2 tsp. kosher salt (divided)
- 4 cups fresh fava beans, shelled
- 2 tbsp. extra-virgin olive oil
- 2 tsp. crushed garlic
- 1/4 tsp. white pepper
- 1/2 tsp. cayenne pepper
- 1 tsp. lemon zest, finely grated
- 2 tsp. freshly squeezed lemon juice

DIRECTIONS:

1. Add 1 teaspoon of salt to a medium-sized pot of water. When the water reaches a rolling boil, boil the fava beans for 3-4 minutes, or until just softened. Strain the beans through a colander set over the sink, before immediately transferring them to a bowl of ice water. Remove the skins once the beans are completely cooled.

2. In a large frying pan over medium-high heat, heat the olive oil. When the oil is nice and hot, add the garlic, and fry for 30 seconds. Add in the beans, and stir for 2 minutes.

3. Add the remaining salt, pepper, cayenne pepper, lemon zest, and lemon juice, stirring until everything is properly combined. Scrape the beans out of the pan, and serve immediately.

Per Serving:
Calories: 576; Total Fat: 9g; Saturated Fat: 1g; Carbohydrates: 88g; Protein: 39g; Sodium: 311mg; Fiber: 38g

POULTRY

LEMON-SIMMERED CHICKEN & ARTICHOKES

COOK TIME: 10-15 MINS | MAKES: 4 SERVINGS

INGREDIENTS:

- 4 boneless chicken breast halves, skins removed
- 1/4 tsp. Himalayan salt
- 1/4 tsp. freshly ground black pepper
- 2 tsp. avocado oil
- 1 tbsp. lemon juice
- 2 tsp. dried crushed oregano
- 1/4 cup Kalamata olives, pitted and halved
- 2/3 cup reduced-sodium chicken stock
- 14 oz. canned, water-packed, quartered artichoke hearts

DIRECTIONS:

1. Season the chicken breasts with the salt and pepper. Add the oil to a large frying pan over medium-high heat. When the oil is nice and hot, brown the chicken on both sides – about 2-4 minutes per side.

2. When the chicken is nicely browned, stir in the lemon juice, oregano, olives, chicken stock, and artichoke hearts. When the stock begins to boil, reduce the heat, and simmer with a lid on the pan for 4-5 minutes, or until the chicken is properly cooked.

3. Serve hot.

Per Serving:
Calories: 225; Total Fat: 9g; Saturated Fat: 1g; Carbohydrates: 9g; Protein: 26g; Sodium: 864g; Fiber: 0g

CRISPY CHICKEN & CABBAGE NOODLES

COOK TIME: 30-60 MINS | MAKES: 4 SERVINGS

INGREDIENTS:

- Zest of 1/2 small lemon
- 2 tbsp. extra-virgin olive oil
- Himalayan salt
- Freshly ground black pepper
- 2 large chicken thighs, cubed
- 4 tbsp. avocado oil (divided)
- 1 tsp. crushed garlic
- 1/2 small shallot, diced
- 1 cup button mushrooms, sliced
- 1 cup reduced-sodium chicken broth
- 1/2 cup full-fat cream
- 2 tbsp. fresh tarragon, chopped
- 1 tbsp. freshly squeezed lemon juice
- 3/4 to 1 cup water (divided)
- 3 oz. bacon slices, cut into strips
- 1 small head savoy cabbage, cored, and sliced into noodles

DIRECTIONS:

1. In a large bowl, whisk together the lemon zest, olive oil, and a large pinch each of salt and pepper. Add the chicken cubes, and toss to coat. Cover the bowl, and chill for a minimum of two hours, or overnight.

2. In a large frying pan over medium heat, heat 2 tablespoons of avocado oil, before adding the garlic and shallots, and frying for 3-5 minutes, or until the shallots become translucent. Scrape the bowl of chicken cubes, along with the sauce, into the pan, and cook for 8 minutes, stirring at regular intervals to prevent burning.

3. Stir in the mushrooms, and cook for 4-5 minutes before stirring in the chicken broth, and bringing the pan to a boil. Simmer for 5 minutes while stirring. Stir in the cream, and simmer for an additional 5 minutes. Add the tarragon and lemon juice to the pan, and stir, before seasoning to taste with salt and pepper. Transfer the pan to a wooden chopping board, and keep warm.

4. Add 1/2 cup water to a clean frying pan, along with the bacon strips. Bring the bacon to a rolling boil over medium-high heat, boiling for 5-8 minutes, or until the water has reduced, and the bacon is crisp. Use a slotted spoon to transfer the crisped bacon to a plate, and tent with foil.

5. Wipe the pan clean, and add the remaining avocado oil. Heat the oil over medium-high heat, when the oil is nice and hot, add the cabbage, and toss for about 30 seconds. Pour in the remaining water, and season to taste with salt and pepper. Place a lid on the pan, and simmer the cabbage for 8-12 minutes, or until just properly cooked, but still crisp.

6. Transfer the pan to a wooden chopping board, and stir in the crispy bacon. Serve the cooked chicken on a bed of crispy bacon and cabbage noodles.

Tip: Any leftovers can be refrigerated in an airtight container for no more than 4 days.

Per Serving:
Calories: 572; Total Fat: 44.3g; Saturated Fat; 13.5g; Carbohydrates: 6.7g; Protein: 33g; Fiber: 5.1g

OUZO & ORANGE GLAZED DUCK

COOK TIME: 15 MINS | MAKES: 4 SERVINGS

INGREDIENTS:

- 2 duck breast halves
- 1 tsp. flaky sea salt (plus a pinch)
- 1 tbsp. extra-virgin olive oil
- 1/2 cup fennel bulbs, chopped (fronds reserved for topping)
- 1 bird's eye chili, halved and seeded
- 1 small red onion, diced
- 1/4 cup ouzo
- 1/2 cup freshly squeezed orange juice
- 1 cup chicken stock
- Freshly ground black pepper

DIRECTIONS:

1. Place the duck breast halves on a wooden chopping board, skin sides up. Using a sharp paring knife, slit a large X across each breast, cutting through the skin and fat, but not into the meat. Rub the salt into the breasts, and let stand on the counter for 5 minutes.

2. In a large pan over medium heat, heat the olive oil. When the oil is nice and hot, add the breasts to the pan, skin side down, and sear for 8-10 minutes. Use tongs to flip the breasts, and sear the bottom halves for an additional 3 minutes. Transfer the seared breasts to a bowl, and keep warm. They need to stand for about 10 minutes while you prepare the rest of the dish.

3. Meanwhile, add the fennel bulbs, chili, and onion to the same pan, and fry for about 3 minutes, or until the vegetables soften. Transfer the pan to a wooden chopping board, and carefully add the ouzo. Use extreme caution during this step, so that the pan does not catch fire. Carefully return the pan to the heat, and use a wooden spoon to stir the contents of the pan, loosening any bits of food that have stuck to the bottom. The ouzo should reduce to about half.

4. Stir the orange juice and stock into the pan, along with an extra pinch of salt. Allow the sauce to boil for 5 minutes while stirring, until the sauce is thick enough to coat the back of a wooden spoon. Turn off the heat.

5. Working against the grain, slice the duck breasts into 1/8-inch thick slices. Plate the slices, and serve topped with the sauce and reserved fennel fronds, while still warm.

Per Serving:
Calories: 229; Total Fat: 9g; Saturated Fat: 1g; Carbohydrates: 7g; Protein: 27g; Sodium: 781mg; Fiber: 1g

ZESTY, LETTUCE-WRAPPED CHICKEN GYROS

COOK TIME: 30 MINS | MAKES: 4 SERVINGS

INGREDIENTS:

- 1 1/2 lbs. boneless chicken breasts, skins removed
- 1/2 tsp. white pepper
- 1/2 tsp. kosher salt
- 1/2 tsp. dried thyme
- 1/2 tsp. dried oregano
- 1/2 tsp. ground cumin
- 1 tsp. crushed garlic
- 2 tbsp. freshly squeezed lemon juice
- 1 lemon, zested
- 8 outer leaves of romaine lettuce
- Tahini sauce
- 4 thin dill pickle spears
- Very thinly sliced red onion
- 1 heirloom tomato, sliced

DIRECTIONS:

1. Place the chicken breasts on a wooden chopping board, and cover with greaseproof paper. Pound the breasts, using a wooden mallet, to about 1/4-inches thick, before slicing into 6 strips.

2. In a large bowl, whisk together the pepper, salt, thyme, oregano, cumin, garlic, lemon juice, and lemon zest. Add the chicken strips, and toss to coat. Cover the bowl in cling wrap, and chill overnight, or for a minimum of 30 minutes.

3. When the chicken is properly chilled, preheat the oven broiler on low, with the wire rack about 6-inches away from the broiler. Arrange the chicken strips on a foil-covered baking sheet, and broil in the oven for 7 minutes, or until the chicken is just properly cooked.

4. Place the lettuce leaves on a plate, and top each leaf with a generous dollop of tahini sauce, followed by the dill spears, red onions, and tomato slices. Divide the cooked chicken between the leaves, fold, and serve.

Per Serving:
Calories: 150; Total Fat: 3g; Carbohydrates: 2g; Protein: 26g; Sodium: 280mg; Fiber: 1g

GROUND TURKEY PATTIES IN GREEN SAUCE

COOK TIME: 20-30 MINS | MAKES: 16 SERVINGS

INGREDIENTS:

- 3/4 cups extra-virgin olive oil
- 2 tbsp. freshly squeezed lemon juice
- 3 tbsp. balsamic vinegar
- 2 tsp. crushed garlic
- 4 pieces canned anchovies, drained
- 2 tbsp. capers
- 1/4 cup fresh mint leaves, chopped
- 2 cups fresh parsley leaves, packed
- 1 cup fresh basil leaves, packed

- Himalayan salt
- Freshly ground black pepper
- 1 tbsp. extra-virgin avocado oil (more if needed)
- 1 tsp. fresh thyme leaves
- 1 small shallot, chopped
- 3 tbsp. coconut flour
- 1 lemon, zested
- 1 large free-range egg
- 1 lb. lean ground turkey

DIRECTIONS:

1. In a food processor, pulse the olive oil, lemon juice, vinegar, garlic, anchovies, capers, mint leaves, parsley, and basil on high, until you have a lump-free paste. Season to taste with salt and pepper, before scraping half of the mixture into a bowl, and covering to chill while you prepare the rest of the dish. The remainder of the sauce can be kept in the fridge in an airtight container, for no more than 2 weeks.

2. In a small frying pan over medium heat, heat the avocado oil before frying the thyme leaves and shallots for about 3 minutes, or until the shallots just begin to soften. Remove the pan from the heat, and scrape the shallots and thyme into a large serving bowl. Allow to cool slightly.

3. When the shallots have cooled slightly, add the coconut flour, zest, egg, and turkey to the bowl, along with 1/2 teaspoon each of salt and pepper. Use clean hands to properly combine all of the ingredients. Form the meat into 16 patties, and fry in batches of four or more (using the same pan you used to fry the shallots), for about 8 minutes per side. Transfer the cooked patties to a serving platter, and keep warm. Repeat the process with the remaining patties, adding a bit of extra avocado oil to the pan if needed.

4. Serve the cooked patties hot, with a side of chilled green sauce for dipping.

Per Serving:
Calories: 494; Total Fat: 41.9g; Saturated Fat: 8.8g; Carbohydrates: 2.8g; Protein: 25g; Fiber: 1.9g

HERB-MARINATED CHICKEN & RADISH SALAD

COOK TIME: 50 MINS | MAKES: 4 SERVINGS

INGREDIENTS:

- 4 boneless chicken breast halves, skins removed
- Himalayan salt
- Freshly ground black pepper
- 2/3 cup Moroccan chermoula
- 1 cup fresh parsley leaves, chopped
- 1/4 red onion, thinly sliced
- 1 English cucumber, thinly sliced
- 12 small radishes, thinly sliced
- 2 tbsp. extra-virgin olive oil
- 1 tbsp. freshly squeezed lemon juice
- 1 tbsp. lightly toasted sesame seeds

DIRECTIONS:

1. Place the chicken breasts on a wooden chopping board, and use a sharp knife to cut a few small slits into them. Massage the breasts with a generous pinch of salt and pepper, before placing them in a bowl. Coat the breasts with the chermoula, and chill covered for at least an hour, or overnight.

2. Set the oven to preheat to 400°F, with the wire rack in the center of the oven.

3. Place the marinated chicken, along with the marinade, in an oven dish, and bake for 45-50 minutes, or until the chicken is properly cooked. Allow the chicken to rest on the countertop while you prepare the salad.

4. In a large bowl, gently toss together the parsley, onion, cucumber, and radishes. Add the olive oil, lemon juice, and 1/4 teaspoon each of salt and pepper to the bowl, tossing until all of the ingredients are evenly coated.

5. Serve the chicken on a bed of the radish salad, and garnish with the sesame seeds before serving.

Per Serving:
Calories: 426; Total Fat: 30g; Saturated Fat: 5g; Carbohydrates: 7g; Protein: 35g; Sodium: 411mg; Fiber: 2g

CURRIED CHICKEN PATTIES

COOK TIME: 15-20 MINS | MAKES: 4 SERVINGS

INGREDIENTS:

- 1/3 tsp. freshly ground black pepper
- 1/4 tsp. kosher salt
- 1/2 tsp. ground turmeric powder
- 1 tsp. ground ginger
- 1 tsp. crushed garlic
- 1/4 cup shallots, finely chopped
- 1 lb. ground chicken
- 1 tbsp. avocado oil (more if needed)

DIRECTIONS:

1. Add the pepper, salt, turmeric, ginger, garlic, shallots, and chicken to a large mixing bowl, and stir until all of the ingredients are properly combined. Form the chicken into 8 patties of roughly the same size.

2. In a large frying pan over medium heat, heat 1 tablespoon of the avocado oil. When the oil is hot, fry the patties in batches. Fry for 2-3 minutes per side, until the patties are nicely browned on both sides. Add extra oil to the pan as needed between batches.

3. Serve the patties hot, on buns of your choice.

Per Serving:
Calories: 206; Total Fat: 14g; Carbohydrates: 1g; Protein: 20g; Sodium: 213mg; Fiber: 0g

CURRIED DUCK & WINTER VEGETABLES

COOK TIME: 1-2 HOURS | MAKES: 4 SERVINGS

INGREDIENTS:

- 1 lb. duck legs or drumsticks
- 1 tsp. crushed garlic
- Himalayan salt
- Freshly ground black pepper
- 1/8 tsp. ground cardamom
- 1/8 tsp. red pepper flakes
- 1/4 tsp. ground turmeric powder
- 1/4 tsp. sweet smoked paprika
- 1/4 tsp. ground cilantro seeds
- 1/4 tsp. ground cumin
- 1/4 tsp. ground ginger
- 3 tbsp. extra-virgin olive oil
- 5.3 oz. chopped cavolo Nero kale, stems removed
- 3 cups Brussels sprouts, halved and trimmed

DIRECTIONS:

1. Set the oven to preheat to 355°F, with the wire rack in the center of the oven.

2. Place the duck legs on a wooden chopping board, and use a sharp paring knife to cut small slits into the skins and fat. Massage the duck with the garlic, and season with a large pinch of salt and pepper. Place the seasoned duck legs in a large mixing bowl.

3. In a small glass bowl, whisk together the cardamom, red pepper flakes, turmeric, smoked paprika, cilantro seeds, cumin, and ginger. Add the spices to the bowl of duck legs, and toss to coat. Arrange the coated duck legs on a baking tray, and sprinkle with the olive oil. Bake in the oven for 1 hour and 10 minutes, turning the legs over halfway through the cooking time.

4. When the duck legs are properly cooked, transfer to a serving platter, and keep warm.

5. Add the kale and Brussels sprouts to the pan, and stir through the rendered duck fat, until evenly coated. Return the tray to the oven, and bake for 15-20 minutes, or until the vegetables are tender and crisp.

6. Serve the cooked vegetables alongside the warm duck legs on the serving platter.

Tip: Any leftovers can be refrigerated in an airtight container, for no more than 4 days.

Per Serving:
Calories: 658; Total Fat: 56.6g; Saturated Fat: 14.8g; Carbohydrates: 8.6g; Protein: 27.3g; Fiber: 7.6g

STIR-FRIED CHICKEN & BARLEY

COOK TIME: 15 MINS | MAKES: 4 SERVINGS

INGREDIENTS:

- 2 cups water
- 1 cup raw quick-cooking barley
- 3 tsp. avocado oil
- 1 lb. boneless chicken breasts, skins removed, cubed
- 1 medium shallot, chopped
- 1/3 tsp. cayenne pepper
- 1/4 tsp. white pepper
- 1/4 tsp. Himalayan salt
- 1/2 tsp. dried basil, crushed
- 1 tsp. dried oregano, crushed
- 2 tsp. crushed garlic
- 2 medium zucchinis, chopped
- 1 tbsp. fresh flat-leaf parsley, chopped
- 1/4 cup Kalamata olives, pitted and halved
- 2 heirloom tomatoes, chopped

DIRECTIONS:

1. Bring 2 cups of water to a rolling boil over medium heat. When the water is boiling, lower the heat to medium-low, and stir in the raw barley. Place a lid on the pot, and simmer for 10-12 minutes, or until the barley is cooked, stirring occasionally. Remove the pot from the heat, and allow to cool for about 5 minutes.

2. Heat 2 teaspoons of oil in a large frying pan over medium heat, and fry the chicken cubes until properly cooked. Transfer to a bowl, and tent with foil to keep in the heat.

3. Add 1 teaspoon of oil to the same pan, and allow to heat. When the oil is nice and hot, fry the shallots for about 3 minutes, or until just softened. Stir in the cayenne pepper, white pepper, salt, basil, oregano, garlic, and zucchini for a few minutes, until the zucchini softens.

4. Stir in the parsley, olives, tomatoes, and chicken. Serve on a bed of cooked barley.

Per Serving:
Calories: 403; Total Fat: 12g; Saturated Fat: 2g; Carbohydrates: 44g; Protein: 31g; Sodium: 498mg; Fiber: 11g

GROUND TURKEY MINCE

COOK TIME: 10-15 MINS | MAKES: 4 SERVINGS

INGREDIENTS:

- 2 tbsp. avocado oil
- 1 lb. lean ground turkey
- 2 tsp. crushed garlic
- 1 medium red bell pepper, seeded and diced
- 1 small shallot, chopped
- 1/2 tsp. ground cumin
- 1/2 tsp. ground cinnamon
- Freshly ground black pepper
- 1/4 tsp. kosher salt
- 2 tbsp. hummus
- 1/4 cup chicken bone broth
- 1 lemon, finely zested
- 1 tbsp. lemon juice
- Fresh parsley, chopped, for garnish

DIRECTIONS:

1. Heat 1 tablespoon of the oil in a large frying pan over medium-high heat. When the oil is nice and hot, add the ground turkey, and fry for about 5 minutes in a single layer, without stirring. After 5 minutes, flip the meat with a spatula, and stir to separate all the bits. Scrape into a bowl, and set aside.

2. Return the pan to medium-low heat, and add the remaining oil. When the oil is nice and hot, fry the garlic, bell peppers, and shallots for about 5 minutes, or until the vegetables are tender. Stir in the cumin and cinnamon for about 30 seconds, before adding the ground turkey back to the pan, along with a large pinch of pepper, and the salt, hummus, chicken broth, lemon zest, and lemon juice. Stir for 5 minutes.

3. Serve the ground turkey on wraps of your choice, garnished with the fresh parsley.

Per Serving:
Calories: 280; Total Fat: 17g; Carbohydrates: 10g; Protein: 23g; Sodium: 251mg; Fiber: 2g

GREEK-STYLE CHICKEN COUSCOUS

COOK TIME: 3-4 HOURS | MAKES: 6 SERVINGS

INGREDIENTS:

- 1 tbsp. extra-virgin olive oil (plus 1 tsp.)
- 1/2 cup shallots, chopped
- 3 tbsp. crushed garlic
- 6 boneless chicken breast halves, skins removed
- 1 tsp. dried oregano
- 2 tsp. finely grated lemon zest
- 1 tbsp. quick cooking tapioca
- 3 tbsp. sun-dried tomatoes, chopped
- 1/4 cup Kalamata olives, pitted and chopped
- 2 1/2 cups chicken stock (divided)
- 1 3/4 cups raw couscous
- 1/2 cup crumbled feta cheese

DIRECTIONS:

1. Heat 1 tablespoon of oil in a small frying pan over medium heat, before adding the shallots, and frying for 3 minutes, or until the shallots become translucent. Stir in the garlic, and fry for an additional 1 minute.

2. Scrape the cooked shallots and garlic into a large slow cooker, along with the chicken, oregano, zest, tapioca, tomatoes, olives, and a 3/4 cup of chicken stock. With the cooker on the lowest setting, cook the chicken for 3-4 hours, or until it is properly cooked. Shred chicken if desired, or cut into cubes. The chicken may also be left whole.

3. Bring the remaining stock and olive oil to a rolling boil, in a large pot over medium heat. Transfer the pot to a wooden chopping board, and stir in the uncooked couscous. Allow the couscous to stand for about 5 minutes, or until all of the liquid has been absorbed.

4. Serve the cooked chicken on a bed of couscous, topped with the feta cheese

Per Serving:
Calories: 475; Total Fat: 11g; Saturated Fat: 3g; Carbohydrates: 48g; Protein: 44g; Sodium: 683mg; Fiber: 3g

VEGETABLE & HERB CHICKEN CACCIATORE

COOK TIME: 1 HOUR 10 MINS | MAKES: 6-8 SERVINGS

INGREDIENTS:

- 1 cup boiling water
- 1/2 oz. dried porcini mushrooms
- 2 tbsp. avocado oil
- 12 boneless chicken thighs, skins removed and fat trimmed
- 1 large fennel bulb, cored, halved, and thinly sliced
- 1 large shallot, halved and thinly sliced
- 1 large green bell pepper, seeded, and chopped into rings
- 1 tsp. fresh thyme leaves, chopped
- 2 tsp. finely grated orange zest
- 1 tbsp. fresh rosemary, chopped
- 3 tsp. crushed garlic
- 3 tbsp. balsamic vinegar
- 1 tsp. kosher salt
- 2 tbsp. tomato paste
- 3/4 cup dry white wine

DIRECTIONS:

1. Set the oven to preheat to 350°F, with the wire rack in the center of the oven.

2. Place the boiling water and mushrooms in a large bowl, and allow to soak on the counter for 20 minutes.

3. Meanwhile, heat the olive oil in a large frying pan over medium-high heat, before adding the chicken thighs, and browning on all sides. Cook the chicken in batches if needed, to avoid overcrowding the pan. Transfer the cooked thighs to a large casserole dish.

4. Lower the heat, and add the fennel, shallots, and bell pepper to the same pan, frying for about 5 minutes, or until the vegetables are fork-tender. Add the thyme, zest, rosemary, and garlic. Fry for 30 seconds before adding the vinegar, and frying for an additional 1 minute.

5. Finely chop the soaked mushrooms before adding them to the pan, along with the soaking water, salt, tomato paste, and wine.

6. Once the sauce begins to boil, carefully pour the contents of the pan over the thighs in the casserole dish. Cover the dish with foil, and bake for 45 minutes.

7. Allow the cooked thighs to stand on the counter for 5-10 minutes before serving hot.

Per Serving:
Calories: 468; Total Fat: 19g; Saturated Fat: 5g; Carbohydrates: 9g; Protein: 58g; Sodium: 527mg; Fiber: 3g

ITALIAN-STYLE SLOW COOKER CHICKEN

COOK TIME: 5-6 HOURS | MAKES: 6 SERVINGS

INGREDIENTS:

- 1 tsp. white pepper
- 1 tsp. kosher salt
- 1/4 tsp. red pepper flakes
- 2 tsp. sweet smoked paprika
- 3 lbs. boneless chicken breast halves, skins removed
- 14 oz. canned, water-packed artichoke hearts, drained and rinsed
- 1 medium shallot, chopped
- 1 sweet red pepper, chopped
- 1/2 lb. button mushrooms, cleaned, and stems removed
- 2 tbsp. fresh thyme leaves, chopped
- 3 tsp. crushed garlic
- 16 oz. canned tomato paste
- 1 1/2 cups chardonnay
- Hot cooked pasta for serving
- Parmesan cheese, grated, for garnish
- 1/4 cup fresh parsley, chopped, for garnish

DIRECTIONS:

1. In a small glass bowl, whisk together the pepper, salt, red pepper flakes, and paprika. Place the chicken breasts in a large slow cooker, and sprinkle with the spice mixture, using your hands to massage the spice into the chicken in an even layer. Add the artichoke hearts, shallots, sweet red pepper, and mushrooms.

2. In a medium-sized bowl, whisk together the thyme, garlic, tomato paste, and chardonnay, until properly combined. Pour the mixture over everything in the slow cooker.

3. Place the lid on the slow cooker, and cook for 5-6 hours, until the chicken is tender.

4. Serve the chicken and vegetables on a bed of hot pasta, and garnish with parmesan and parsley.

Per Serving:
Calories: 282; Total Fat: 5g; Saturated Fat: 2g; Carbohydrates: 16g; Protein: 43g; Sodium: 550mg; Fiber: 5g

SPICY, YOGURT-MARINATED CHICKEN SKEWERS

COOK TIME: 12 MINS | MAKES: 4-6 SERVINGS

INGREDIENTS:

- 1 1/2 tbsp. Aleppo pepper (extra for garnish)
- 3 tsp. crushed garlic
- 1 tsp. freshly ground black pepper
- 2 tsp. Himalayan salt
- 2 tbsp. tomato paste
- 2 tbsp. balsamic vinegar
- 3 tbsp. extra-virgin olive oil (extra for brushing)
- 1 cup plain Greek yogurt
- 1 3/4 lbs. boneless chicken breasts, skins removed, cubed
- 2 unpeeled lemons, thinly sliced (divided)

DIRECTIONS:

1. Place the Aleppo pepper in a large bowl, along with 1 tablespoon of warm water, and let stand for 5 minutes, until the mixture thickens. Whisk in the garlic, pepper, salt, tomato paste, vinegar, olive oil, and yogurt. Add the chicken cubes, and half of the lemon slices. Toss to coat. Cover the bowl in cling wrap, and chill overnight, or for a minimum of 1 hour.

2. Place 10-12 wooden skewers in a bowl of water, and soak for 20 minutes to prevent charring.

3. Brush a grill with extra olive oil, and heat on medium-high. When the grill is nice and hot. Thread the marinated chicken cubes onto the soaked skewers, discarding the excess marinade. Grill the skewers for 10-12 minutes, turning at regular intervals, until the chicken is cooked all the way through, and nicely browned on all sides.

4. Serve the skewers hot on a bed of lemon slices.

Per Serving:
Calories: 301; Total Fat: 11g; Saturated Fat: 2g; Carbohydrates: 7g; Protein: 44g; Sodium: 1,035mg; Fiber: 1g

ONE-PAN CHICKEN PECAN BAKE

COOK TIME: 30-60 MINS | MAKES: 4 SERVINGS

INGREDIENTS:

- 4 whole garlic cloves
- 1/2 medium shallot, diced
- 1 medium green bell pepper, seeded and diced
- 1 medium red bell pepper, seeded and diced
- 2 lbs. chicken drumsticks
- 2 tbsp. avocado oil
- Freshly ground black pepper
- 1/2 tsp. kosher salt
- 1 tsp. dried basil
- 1 tsp. dried thyme
- 1/2 cup pecan halves
- 2 tbsp. red wine vinegar

DIRECTIONS:

1. Cover a large, rimmed baking pan with greaseproof paper, and set the oven to preheat to 400°F, with the wire rack in the center of the oven.

2. Arrange the garlic, shallots, bell peppers, and drumsticks in a single layer on the prepared baking pan.

3. Sprinkle the oil over everything. Season the contents of the pan with a generous pinch of black pepper, salt, basil, and thyme. Sprinkle the pecans over all.

4. Place the pan in the oven for 30 minutes, flipping the chicken, and stirring the vegetables, halfway through the cooking time. When the vegetables are tender but crisp, and the drumsticks are nicely browned, remove the pan from the oven, and drizzle the vinegar over everything. Stir the vinegar through, and serve hot.

Per Serving:
Calories: 391; Total Fat: 28g; Carbohydrates: 11g; Protein: 27g; Sodium: 42mg; Fiber: 3g

FISH & SEAFOOD

VERY-BERRY SWEET CHILI SALMON FILLETS

COOK TIME: 15 MINS | MAKES: 4 SERVINGS

INGREDIENTS:

- 2 tbsp. sweet chili sauce (divided)
- 1 spring onion, finely chopped
- 1 Persian cucumber, finely chopped
- 1 cup fresh blackberries
- 1 tbsp. avocado oil
- 4 skin-on salmon fillets
- 1/2 tsp. flaky sea salt
- 1/2 tsp. freshly ground black pepper

DIRECTIONS:

1. In a medium-sized mixing bowl, gently stir together 1 tablespoon of sweet chili sauce, and the spring onion, cucumber, and blackberries. Set aside.

2. Brush a grill with 1 tablespoon of avocado oil, and preheat on medium-high. Season the salmon fillets with salt and pepper, before placing them skin down on the heated grill. Place a lid on the grill, and cook the fillets for 2-3 minutes, before brushing them with the remaining chili sauce. Replace the lid, and continue to cook for 10-12 minutes, or until the fillets are opaque.

3. Serve the cooked salmon hot, topped with the blackberry mixture.

Per Serving:
Calories: 303; Total Fat: 16g; Saturated Fat; 3g: Carbohydrates: 9g; Protein: 30g; Sodium: 510mg; Fiber: 2g

GREEK-STYLE PAN-ROASTED SWORDFISH

COOK TIME: 15 MINS | MAKES: 4 SERVINGS

INGREDIENTS:

- 4 tbsp. extra-virgin avocado oil (divided)
- 1 small shallot, thinly sliced
- 2 tsp. crushed garlic
- 1/2 medium eggplant, diced
- 2 medium zucchinis, diced
- 1 cup whole Greek olives, pitted
- 2 cups cherry tomatoes, halved
- 4 skin-on swordfish fillets, patted dry
- Himalayan salt
- Freshly ground black pepper
- 1/4 cup green olive tapenade with harissa

DIRECTIONS:

1. Set the oven to preheat to 375°F, with the wire rack in the center of the oven.

2. Heat 2 tablespoons of oil in a large frying pan over medium-high heat. When the oil is nice and hot, fry the shallots and garlic for about 5 minutes, or until the shallots become translucent. Stir in the eggplant, and fry until it starts to become tender – about 3 minutes. Add the zucchini, and stir for an additional 5 minutes, until all of the vegetables are fork-tender, and crispy around the edges. Stir in the olives and tomatoes, and fry, and stirring for 2 minutes. Set the pan aside, off the heat.

3. Season the fish generously with salt and pepper. Heat the remaining olive oil in an oven-proof pan over medium-high heat. When the oil is nice and hot, place the fish fillets skin down in the pan, and fry for 3 minutes. The edges should just begin to become solid. Flip the fish in the pan before transferring to the oven, and baking for a final 3 minutes. The fish should be completely solid and flaky when done.

4. Top the cooked swordfish with fried vegetables and olive tapenade. Serve immediately.

Per Serving: Calories: 605; Total Fat: 37g; Saturated Fat: 6g; Sodium: 738mg; Carbohydrates: 16g; Fiber: 6g; Protein: 54g

GARLIC BROILED FLOUNDER FILLETS

COOK TIME: 24 MINS | MAKES: 4 SERVINGS

INGREDIENTS:

- 1/4 tsp. Himalayan salt
- 1 tsp. freshly ground black pepper
- 1 tsp. crushed garlic
- 1 lemon, zested (segments reserved for garnish)
- 1 tbsp. avocado oil
- 4 flounder fillets, patted dry
- 1 tsp. capers, chopped
- 1/4 cup fresh parsley, chopped

DIRECTIONS:

1. Line a large, rimmed baking tray with tin foil, and lightly coat with cooking spray. Set the oven broiler to preheat on low, with the wire rack about 6-inches away from the broiler.

2. In a small glass bowl, whisk together the salt, pepper, garlic, lemon zest, and avocado oil. Place the flounder fillets on the prepared baking tray, and brush with the oil mixture. Place the tray in the oven for about 10 minutes, or until the fish is no longer see-through. Broiler time may vary depending on the thickness of the fillets.

3. Plate the broiled fish, and garnish with the capers, parsley, and reserved lemon segments before serving.

Per Serving:
Calories: 151; Total Fat: 9g; Carbohydrates: 1g; Protein: 16g; Sodium: 456mg; Fiber: 0g

SPICY MACKEREL & KELP BOWLS

COOK TIME: 15-20 MINS | MAKES: 2 SERVINGS

INGREDIENTS:

- 1 tsp. crushed garlic
- 2 tbsp. tahini
- 3 tbsp. extra-virgin olive oil
- 1 tbsp. freshly squeezed lemon juice
- 1 tbsp. freshly grated ginger
- 2 mackerel fillets
- Himalayan salt
- Freshly ground black pepper
- 1 tbsp. extra-virgin avocado oil
- 1 small bok choy, halved
- 16-20 asparagus spears
- 6 oz. kelp noodles, drained
- 1/4 cup macadamia nuts, roughly chopped
- 1 tbsp. fresh coriander leaves, chopped
- 1 small bird's eye chili, sliced

DIRECTIONS:

1. In a small glass bowl, whisk together the garlic, tahini, 2 tablespoons of olive oil, lemon juice, and ginger. You may add a tablespoon or two of water to thin the sauce out a bit.

2. Score the mackerel skin in 2 or 3 places, before seasoning to taste with salt and pepper.

3. Heat the avocado oil in a large frying pan over medium heat. When the oil is nice and hot, fry the seasoned fillets for 2-3 minutes per side, before transferring them to a dish, and setting aside.

4. Place the bok choy and asparagus spears in a steamer basket or colander with a fitted lid, over a pot of boiling water that is not touching the bottom of the basket or colander. Steam the vegetables for a few minutes, until tender.

5. Serve the cooked mackerel and steamed vegetables on a bed of kelp noodles. Drizzle with the remaining olive oil, and sprinkle with a large pinch each of salt and pepper. Top with the prepared dressing, and sprinkle with chopped nuts, coriander leaves, and chili. Serve hot.

Tip: Any leftovers can be stored in the fridge in an airtight container, for no more than 24 hours.

Per Serving:
Calories: 751; Total Fat: 66.2g; Saturated Fat: 11g; Carbohydrates: 13.3g; Protein: 30.5g; Fiber: 6.5g

TRADITIONAL GREEK WINE-BRAISED OCTOPUS

COOK TIME: 50-60 MINS | MAKES: 4 SERVINGS

INGREDIENTS:

- 2 lbs. uncooked octopus
- Coarse sea salt
- 4 whole bay leaves
- 1 1/2 tsp. crushed fennel seeds
- 1/2 cup dry white wine
- 3 tbsp. white wine vinegar
- 1/2 tsp. cayenne pepper
- 2 tbsp. fresh parsley, chopped
- 1/4 cup freshly squeezed lime juice
- 1/3 cup extra-virgin olive oil

DIRECTIONS:

1. Place the octopus in a colander over the sink, and remove the beak. Massage the whole octopus with a generous amount of coarse sea salt, and rinse until the octopus is completely clean, and no longer slimy.

2. In a large pot, whisk together the bay leaves, fennel seeds, white wine, and white wine vinegar. Place the cleaned octopus in the sauce, and cover with a fitted lid. You don't want any of the liquid to escape from the pot. Bring the wine sauce to a rolling boil over medium heat. When the sauce begins to boil, lower the heat to maintain a very gentle simmer. Simmer the octopus for 50-55 minutes, or until the largest part of a tentacle is tender all the way through. Do not add any extra salt or water to the pot while cooking. When the octopus is properly cooked, transfer to a wooden chopping board, and let stand for about 10 minutes before cutting.

3. While the octopus is cooling, continue to whisk the wine sauce with the pot still on the heat, until the sauce evaporates by about half. Remove the pot from the stove, and allow the sauce to cool to room temperature. Pour the reduced sauce through a fine metal sieve into a bowl, removing and discarding any grit.

4. Add the cayenne pepper, parsley, lime juice, and olive oil to the cooled sauce, and whisk until everything is properly combined.

5. Slice the octopus head and tentacles into thick slices. Toss with the wine sauce, and serve hot with a side of your choice.

Tip: Any leftovers can be stored in the fridge in an airtight container, for no more than 3 days.

Per Serving:
Calories: 576; Total Fat: 43g; Saturated Fat: 6.1g; Carbohydrates: 7.3g; Protein: 33.8g; Fiber: 0.4g

CINNAMON-GLAZED HALIBUT FILLETS

COOK TIME: 20 MINS | MAKES: 4 SERVINGS

INGREDIENTS:

- 1/4 cup extra-virgin avocado oil
- 3/4 tsp. ground cumin
- 1/2 tsp. white pepper (divided)
- 1/2 tsp. kosher salt (divided)
- 1/2 tsp. ground cinnamon
- 1 1/2 tbsp. capers, drained
- 15 oz. canned diced tomatoes, drained
- 4 halibut fillets

DIRECTIONS:

1. Place the oil in a large frying pan over medium heat. When the oil is nice and hot, add the cumin, and fry for about 1 minute, or until fragrant. Stir in 1/4 teaspoon of pepper, 1/4 teaspoon of salt, the cinnamon, capers, and canned tomatoes. Stir the sauce for about 10 minutes, or until it thickens.

2. Use paper towels to pat the fish dry. Season the fillets on both sides with the remaining salt and pepper. Nestle the seasoned fillets in the simmering sauce, and cover the pan. Allow the fish to simmer for 8-10 minutes, or until it is opaque, and flakes easily.

3. Plate the fish, and serve immediately, with the sauce ladled over the cooked fish. Enjoy!

Per Serving:
Calories: 309; Total Fat: 14g; Saturated Fat: 2g; Carbohydrates: 5g; Protein: 40g; Sodium: 525mg; Fiber: 2g

AVOCADO-TOSSED SHRIMP SALAD

COOK TIME: 30 MINS | MAKES: 2 SERVINGS

INGREDIENTS:

- 1/2 lb. cooked medium shrimp
- Freshly ground black pepper
- Himalayan salt
- 1/4 tsp. cayenne pepper
- 1 tbsp. mayonnaise
- 1 tbsp. freshly squeezed lemon juice
- 1 spring onion, thinly sliced
- 1 large Hass avocado, peeled, pitted, and diced
- 4 cups baby arugula
- 2 tbsp. balsamic vinegar
- 1 tbsp. extra-virgin olive oil
- 1/2 cup cherry tomatoes, halved
- 1/4 cup shelled pistachios, roughly chopped

DIRECTIONS:

1. Remove the shrimp tails, and discard. Cut each shrimp into 3 sections, before placing them in a large bowl. Season the shrimp with a few grinds of pepper, and 1/8 teaspoon of salt. Add the cayenne pepper, mayonnaise, lemon juice, and spring onions, stirring until all of the ingredients are properly combined. Stir in the avocado until just combined. Do not over stir.

2. Place the arugula in a large salad bowl, and toss with the vinegar and olive oil. Season to taste with salt and pepper.

3. Serve the shrimp on the bed of seasoned arugula, garnished with chopped pistachios and tomatoes.

Per Serving:
Calories: 293; Total Fat: 20g; Carbohydrates: 11g; Protein: 21g; Sodium: 765mg; Fiber: 6g

HEALTHY TUNA & BEAN WRAPS

COOK TIME: 0 MINS | MAKES: 4 SERVINGS

INGREDIENTS:

- 15 oz. canned cannellini beans, drained and rinsed
- 12 oz. canned light tuna in water, drained and flaked
- 1/8 tsp. white pepper
- 1/8 tsp. kosher salt
- 1 tbsp. fresh parsley, chopped
- 2 tbsp. extra-virgin avocado oil
- 1/4 cup red onion, chopped
- 12 romaine lettuce leaves
- 1 medium-sized ripe Hass avocado, sliced

DIRECTIONS:

1. In a large mixing bowl, stir together the beans, tuna, pepper, salt, parsley, avocado oil, and red onions.

2. Spoon some of the mixture onto each lettuce leaf, and top with the sliced avocado before folding and serving.

Per Serving:
Calories: 279; Total Fat: 13g; Saturated Fat: 2g; Carbohydrates: 19g; Protein: 22g; Sodium: 421g; Fiber: 7g

COCONUT-MARINATED SALMON BOWLS

COOK TIMES: 10 MINS | MAKES: 2 SERVINGS

INGREDIENTS:

- 2 medium scallions, sliced
- 1 tbsp. sesame seeds
- 1/2 tsp. cayenne pepper
- 1 tsp. toasted sesame oil
- 2 tbsp. extra-virgin olive oil (plus 2 tsp.)
- 1 tbsp. coconut aminos
- 8 oz. sushi-grade wild salmon, cut into small cubes
- 1/2 medium cauliflower
- 2 tbsp. extra-virgin avocado oil
- 1 tbsp. freshly squeezed lemon juice
- Kosher salt
- White pepper
- 1 medium English cucumber, cubed
- 1 large avocado, cubed
- 1/2 nori sheet, cut into small pieces

DIRECTIONS:

1. In a medium-sized bowl, whisk together the scallions, sesame seeds, cayenne pepper, toasted sesame oil, 2 tablespoons of olive oil, and coconut aminos. Add the salmon cubes, and toss to coat. Set aside on the counter while you prepare the rest of the dish.

2. Break the cauliflower into florets, and pulse on high in a blender until the chunks resemble rice. Heat the avocado oil in a large frying pan over medium heat. When the oil is nice and hot, add the cauliflower rice, and toss for 5-7 minutes. Transfer the pan to a wooden chopping board, and toss in the lemon juice. Season to taste with salt and pepper.

3. Divide the cooked cauliflower rice between 2 bowls, and top with the marinated salmon. Garnish with the cucumber and avocado, before sprinkling with the remaining olive oil and the nori pieces. Serve immediately.

Per Serving:
Calories: 668; Total Fat: 54g; Saturated Fat: 7.8g; Carbohydrates: 20.3g; Protein: 30.9g; Fiber: 11.1g

HERB-INFUSED SEAFOOD PAELLA

COOK TIME: 20-25 MIN | MAKES: 4 SERVINGS

INGREDIENTS:

- Pinch saffron
- 1/4 cup water
- 2.3 oz. calamari rings
- 5.3 oz. uncooked prawns
- 1 tbsp. freshly squeezed lemon juice
- Flaky sea salt
- Freshly ground black pepper
- 2 tbsp. extra-virgin avocado oil
- 2 wild salmon fillets
- 1 medium cauliflower

- 3 tbsp. safflower oil
- 1/2 small shallot
- 4 tsp. crushed garlic
- 1/2 tsp. red pepper flakes
- 1 tsp. sweet smoked paprika
- 2 tbsp. tomato paste
- 1/4 cup chicken broth
- 1/4 cup fresh parsley, chopped
- 6 tbsp. extra virgin olive oil

DIRECTIONS:

1. Place the saffron in 1/4 cup of water, and let stand while you prepare the rest of the dish.

2. In a large bowl, toss together the calamari rings, prawns, and lemon juice. Season to taste with a large pinch of salt and pepper. Set aside. Heat 1 tablespoon of the avocado oil in a large frying pan over medium heat. When the oil is nice and hot, add the salmon to the pan, and fry for 2-3 minutes per side, or until the salmon is nicely browned. Transfer the cooked salmon to a plate, and use a fork to flake the fish into small pieces.

3. Add the remaining avocado oil to the same pan, and fry the seasoned calamari and prawns for 2-3 minutes, or until properly cooked. Scrape the cooked seafood into a bowl, and set aside, tenting to keep warm.

4. Break the cauliflower into florets, and process on high in a blender, until the pieces resemble rice. Add the safflower oil to the pan, and heat over medium-high heat. When the oil is nice and hot, fry the shallots for 5 minutes, or until translucent. Add the garlic, and fry for 1 additional minute. Whisk in the soaked saffron with the 1/4 cup of water. Add the red pepper flakes, paprika, tomato paste, broth, and cauliflower rice, stirring until all of the ingredients are properly combined. Cook the broth for 5-7 minutes, or until the cauliflower has just softened, but still remains crisp.

5. Add the flaked salmon, calamari, and prawns to the pan of sauce, stirring for 1-2 minutes, until the fish is heated through. Transfer the pan to a wooden chopping board, and stir in half of the chopped parsley. Scrape the paella into a serving bowl, and garnish with the remaining parsley. Drizzle with the olive oil, and serve warm.

Tip: Any leftover paella can be refrigerated in an airtight container, for no more than 4 days.

Per Serving:
Calories: 564; Total Fat: 44g; Saturated Fat: 6.4g; Carbohydrates: 13g; Protein: 31.7g; Fiber: 4.1g

TWO-WAY TILAPIA FILLETS

COOK TIME: 15-20 MINS | MAKES: 6 SERVINGS

INGREDIENTS:

- 6 tilapia fillets
- 2 cups diced tomatoes
- 1 tsp. crushed oregano
- 1 tsp. crushed sweet basil
- 2 tsp. crushed garlic flakes
- 1/2 cup roasted sweet peppers, chopped
- 1/4 cup button mushrooms, sliced
- 1/2 cup mozzarella, grated
- 1/2 cup Kalamata olives, pitted and diced
- 1 whole avocado, sliced
- 1/2 cup frozen corn (thawed)
- 1/2 cup feta cheese, crumbled
- 1 tsp. fresh coriander leaves, chopped

DIRECTIONS:

1. Set the oven to preheat to 400°F, with the wire rack in the center of the oven. Coat a large, rimmed baking tray with cooking spray.

2. Place the tilapia fillets on the prepared baking sheet, 3 per side. Divide the crushed tomatoes between the 6 fillets, using the back of a spoon to spread it out in an even layer. Top 3 of the fillets with oregano, sweet basil, crushed garlic, roasted sweet peppers, mushrooms, and mozzarella.

3. Top each of the remaining fillets with the olives, avocado, corn, feta, and fresh coriander.

4. Bake the fish in the oven for 15-20 minutes, or until the fish is completely opaque.

5. Serve hot.

Per Serving:
Calories: 197; Total Fat: 4g; Saturated Fat: 2g; Carbohydrates: 5g; Protein: 34g; Sodium: 446mg; Fiber: 1g

MEDITERRANEAN-STUFFED CALAMARI TUBES

COOK TIME: 30 MINS | MAKES: 4-6 SERVINGS

INGREDIENTS:

- 1/2 cup, plus 4 tbsp., extra-virgin olive oil (divided)
- 2 medium shallots, finely chopped
- 1 cup raisins
- 6 cups panko breadcrumbs
- 3/4 cup fresh parsley, finely chopped (divided)
- 1 1/4 cups parmesan cheese, grated (divided)
- 4 tsp. crushed garlic in oil

- 12 large squid tubes, cleaned
- 4 whole garlic cloves, finely chopped
- 28 oz. canned crushed tomatoes
- 1 tsp. kosher salt
- 1 tsp. white pepper
- 1/2 cup fresh basil, finely chopped
- 1 tsp. crushed dried oregano

DIRECTIONS:

1. Set the oven to preheat to 350°F, with the wire rack in the center of the oven.

2. In a large frying pan over medium-high heat, heat 2 tablespoons of oil. When the oil is nice and hot, fry the shallots for about 5 minutes, or until they soften and become translucent. Scrape the shallots into a large bowl. Add 1/2 cup of olive oil, 1 cup raisins, 6 cups breadcrumbs, 1/2 cup parsley, 1 cup parmesan, and 4 teaspoons of garlic, stirring until all of the ingredients are properly combined.

3. Use 1 tablespoon of the oil to grease the inside of a large casserole dish. Use a teaspoon to stuff some of the breadcrumb mixture into each individual squid tube. Use toothpicks to secure the openings, and prevent the stuffing from spilling out while baking. Arrange the stuffed tubes in the prepared casserole dish in a single layer. Place the dish in the preheated oven for 10 minutes.

4. Meanwhile, in a large frying pan over medium-high heat, heat the remaining 2 tablespoons of olive oil. When the oil is nice and hot, fry the garlic for 30 seconds. Stir in the tomatoes, salt, pepper, basil, and oregano. Simmer the sauce for 5 minutes while stirring, allowing the flavors to meld.

5. Transfer the casserole dish to a wooden chopping board, and scrape the sauce over all of the stuffed tubes. Garnish the sauce with the remaining cheese and parsley, before returning the dish to the oven, and baking for an additional 10 minutes. Serve hot.

Per Serving:
Calories: 1,304; Total Fat: 49g; Saturated Fat: 17g; Carbohydrates: 150g; Protein: 67g; Sodium: 4,221mg; Fiber: 19g

ASIAN-STYLE COD BAKE

COOK TIME: 20-25 MINS | MAKES: 4 SERVINGS

INGREDIENTS:

- 1/4 tsp. white pepper
- 1/2 tsp. kosher salt
- 1/4 tsp. ground ginger
- 1 tbsp. coconut aminos
- 2 tsp. crushed garlic
- 1 tsp. toasted sesame oil
- 1/2 cup extra-virgin olive oil
- 3 tbsp. freshly squeezed lemon juice
- 4 cod fillets
- 1.3 lbs. broccoli
- 1 small bird's eye chili, sliced
- Fresh coriander leaves, chopped, for garnish

DIRECTIONS:

1. In a small glass bowl, whisk together the pepper, salt, ginger, coconut aminos, garlic, sesame oil, olive oil, and lemon juice. Set aside.

2. Place the cod fillets in a large mixing bowl, add half of the marinade, and toss to coat. Cover the bowl in cling wrap, and chill for a minimum of 30 minutes. Keep the other half of the marinade for later.

3. Set the oven to preheat to 350°F, with the wire rack in the center of the oven.

4. Slice the broccoli into either florets or bite-sized pieces of even sizes. This will ensure that the broccoli cooks evenly, and doesn't burn. Coat the sliced broccoli with the reserved marinade before arranging it on a baking tray. Pour any excess marinade over all the broccoli on the tray. Bake in the oven for 10-12 minutes.

5. Remove the tray from the oven, and raise the temperature to 400°F. Add the chilled fish, along with all of the marinade and the sliced chili, to the pan of broccoli, and stir. Return the pan to the oven, and bake for 7-10 minutes, or until the fish is completely opaque and flaky.

6. Plate the fish and broccoli, and garnish with the chopped coriander leaves before serving.

Tip: Any leftovers can be refrigerated in an airtight container, for no more than 3 days.

Per Serving:
Calories: 433; Total Fat: 30g; Saturated Fat: 3.6g; Carbohydrates: 12.2g; Protein: 31.2g; Fiber: 4.1g

OLIVE BAKED COD FILLETS

COOK TIME: 15-20 MINS | MAKES: 4 SERVINGS

INGREDIENTS:

- 4 cod fillets
- 2 tbsp. extra-virgin avocado oil
- 1/4 tsp. kosher salt
- 1/8 tsp. white pepper
- 1/2 small shallot, thinly sliced
- 1 small green pepper, thinly sliced
- 1/4 cup Kalamata olives, pitted and chopped
- 8 oz. canned tomato sauce
- 1/4 cup mozzarella cheese, grated

DIRECTIONS:

1. Set the oven to preheat to 400°F, with the wire rack in the center of the oven. Coat a large casserole dish with baking spray.

2. Arrange the cod fillets in the prepared casserole dish. Use a basting brush to coat the fillets with the oil, and season with the salt and pepper. Top the seasoned fillets with the shallots, green peppers, and olives. Pour the tomato sauce over everything in the dish, and top with the cheese.

3. Bake in the oven for 15-20 minutes, or until the fish is flaky and opaque.

Per Serving:
Calories: 246; Total Fat: 12g; Saturated Fat: 2g; Carbohydrates: 6g; Protein: 29g; Sodium: 706mg; Fiber: 2g

ZESTY SCALLOPS & PASTA

COOK TIME: 10-15 MINS | MAKES: 2 SERVINGS

INGREDIENTS:

- 4 oz. raw fettuccine
- 1 tbsp. extra-virgin avocado oil
- 1/4 tsp. cayenne pepper
- 1/2 tsp. lemon zest, finely grated
- 1 tsp. crushed garlic
- 1/2 medium sweet red pepper, julienned
- 1 tbsp. freshly squeezed lemon juice
- 1/4 cup white wine
- 1/2 cup low-sodium chicken stock
- 6 sea scallops
- 2 tsp. parmesan cheese, grated

DIRECTIONS:

1. Prepare the fettuccine according to the instructions on the packaging, and set aside.

2. While the pasta cooks, heat the avocado oil in a large frying pan over medium-high heat. When the oil is nice and hot, add the cayenne pepper, lemon zest, garlic, and sweet red pepper, frying for 2 minutes. Whisk in the lemon juice, white wine, and chicken stock. When the stock begins to boil, lower the heat, and simmer uncovered for 5-6 minutes, or until half of the liquid has evaporated.

3. Halve the scallops horizontally before adding them to the simmering sauce. Cover and cook, stirring at regular intervals for 4-5 minutes, or until the scallops are no longer translucent.

4. Serve the cooked scallops and sauce on a bed of cooked fettuccine, and garnish with the parmesan before serving.

Per Serving:
Calories: 421; Total Fat: 10g; Saturated Fat: 2g; Carbohydrates: 49g; Protein: 30g; Sodium: 861mg; Fiber: 3g

VEGETARIAN

YAM & BEAN BOWLS

COOK TIME: 30-40 MINS | MAKES: 4 SERVINGS

INGREDIENTS:

- 1 1/2 cups water
- 1/4 tsp. garlic salt
- 3/4 cup brown basmati rice
- 3 tbsp. extra-virgin avocado oil (divided)
- 1 large yam, peeled and diced
- 1 medium shallot, finely chopped
- 4 cups spinach, stems removed
- 15 oz. canned turtle beans, drained and rinsed
- 2 tbsp. sweet chili sauce
- lemon wedges for serving

DIRECTIONS:

1. In a large pot over medium-high heat, bring the water, garlic salt, and rice to a boil. Once the water begins to boil, lower the heat, and simmer the rice with a lid on the pot until tender – about 15-20 minutes. Transfer the pot to a wooden chopping board, and allow the rice to rest for 5 minutes.

2. In a large frying pan over medium-high heat, heat 2 tablespoons of the avocado oil. When the oil is nice and hot, add the yams, and toss for about 8 minutes. Stir in the shallots, and toss for an additional 4-6 minutes, or until the yams are fork-tender. Add in the spinach, and cook until the leaves wilt – about 3-5 minutes. Stir in the beans until just heated through.

3. Add the remaining oil, and the sweet chili sauce, stirring to combine. Add the contents of the pan to the cooked rice, and stir.

4. Spoon the rice and beans into bowls, and serve with the lemon wedges on the side.

Per Serving:
Calories: 435; Total Fat: 11g; Saturated Fat: 2g; Carbohydrates: 74g; Protein: 10g; Sodium: 405mg; Fiber: 8g

WHITE BEAN, ZUCCHINI, & SQUASH CASSEROLE

COOK TIME: 1 HOUR | MAKES: 6 SERVINGS

INGREDIENTS:

- 1 small butternut squash
- 1 tsp. freshly ground black pepper
- 1/2 tsp. kosher salt
- 1 tsp. crushed dried oregano
- 1 tsp. crushed garlic
- 1 tbsp. freshly squeezed lemon juice
- 1 tbsp. nutritional yeast
- Extra-virgin olive oil
- 8 oz. canned tomato sauce
- 1/4 medium shallot, diced
- 1 medium zucchini, diced
- 2 cups frozen lima beans, thawed
- 4 oz. Swiss goat cheese, grated
- Fresh coriander leaves for garnish

DIRECTIONS:

1. Set the oven to preheat to 375°F, with the wire rack in the center of the oven. Coat a large casserole dish with olive oil spray.

2. Use a fork to prick tiny holes all over the squash skin. Trim the ends off the squash, and cut in half lengthwise. Remove the seeds before microwaving on high for 1 minute. Remove the skin, and dice the squash into bite-sized cubes. Transfer the cubes to a large mixing bowl.

3. Add the pepper, salt, oregano, garlic, lemon juice, yeast, 1 teaspoon of olive oil, tomato sauce, shallots, zucchini, and lima beans to the bowl, stirring to combine.

4. Stir in the cheese. Scrape the mixture into the prepared casserole dish. Cover the dish with tin foil, and place in the oven for 30-40 minutes, or until the cheese and sauce is bubbling, and the vegetables are fork-tender.

5. When the casserole is done, garnish with the chopped coriander leaves, and drizzle with a few splashes of olive oil before serving hot.

Per Serving:
Calories: 176; Total Fat: 7g; Carbohydrates: 22g; Protein: 9g; Sodium: 295mg; Fiber: 5g

CRISPY VEGETABLE PAELLA

COOK TIME: 35 MINS | MAKES: 4 SERVINGS

INGREDIENTS:

- 3 tbsp. warm water
- 8 threads of fresh saffron
- 3 cups vegetable stock
- 1 tbsp. extra-virgin avocado oil
- 1 large shallot, thinly sliced
- 4 tsp. crushed garlic
- 1 red bell pepper, thinly sliced
- 1 tsp. kosher salt

- 1/2 tsp. freshly ground black pepper
- 2 tbsp. tomato paste
- 3/4 cups canned crushed tomatoes
- 1 1/2 tsp. sweet smoked paprika
- 1 cup uncooked white rice
- 15 oz. canned chickpeas, drained and rinsed
- 1 1/2 cups haricot verts, trimmed and halved
- 1 lime, cut into wedges, for serving

DIRECTIONS:

1. Gently stir together the warm water and saffron in a small glass bowl. Let stand on the counter while you prepare the rest of the dish.

2. Bring the vegetable stock to a simmer in a medium pot over medium-high heat. Once the stock begins to simmer, lower the heat to maintain a very gentle simmer.

3. Heat the avocado oil in a large frying pan over medium-high heat. Stir in the shallots, and fry for about 5 minutes, or until just softened and translucent. Add the garlic, and stir for an additional 30 seconds, allowing the flavors to meld. Toss in the peppers, and continue to fry for about 7 minutes, until the peppers are tender. Add the saffron, along with its soaking water, salt, pepper, tomato paste, crushed tomatoes, and sweet smoked paprika, stirring to combine.

4. Stir in the warm broth, along with the uncooked rice, chickpeas, and haricot verts. Once the mixture begins to boil over medium-high heat, lower the heat, and simmer with the lid off the pan for about 20 minutes, or until the rice is cooked, and the liquid has reduced.

5. Ladle the cooked rice and vegetables into bowls, and serve hot with the lime wedges on the side.

Per Serving:
Calories: 709; Total Fat: 12g; Saturated Fat: 2g; Carbohydrates: 121g; Protein: 33g; Sodium: 1,248mg; Fiber: 22g

ONE-POT CURRIED HALLOUMI

COOK TIME: 20-30 MINS | MAKES: 4 SERVINGS

INGREDIENTS:

- 2 tbsp. extra-virgin olive oil
- 2 packs halloumi cheese
- 1 cup water
- 1/2 cup coconut milk
- 1/4 cup tomato paste
- 1/4 tsp. white pepper
- 1/2 tsp. ground turmeric
- 1 1/2 tsp. mild curry powder
- 1/2 tsp. garlic powder
- 1 tsp. onion powder
- 1 small cauliflower, cut into small florets
- Himalayan salt
- 2 tbsp. coconut flour
- Fresh coriander leaves, chopped, for serving
- Cooked rice for serving

DIRECTIONS:

1. In a large frying pan over medium-high heat, heat the olive oil. Chop the halloumi into 8 slices, about 3/4-inch thick. When the oil is nice and hot, add the halloumi to the pan. You may work in batches if all of the cheese does not fit comfortably in the pan. Fry the halloumi on all sides until golden brown. Don't stress if the cheese is difficult to turn at first, it will become easier the crispier the outer coating becomes. Transfer to a platter, and keep warm.

2. In the same frying pan, stir in the water, coconut milk, tomato paste, pepper, turmeric, curry powder, garlic powder, and onion powder. When the sauce begins to boil, add the cauliflower florets, and season to taste with salt. Simmer the florets for 7-10 minutes with the lid on the pan, or until the cauliflower is fork-tender.

3. When the cauliflower is tender, add the coconut flour to the pan, and stir until the sauce thickens. Stir in the cooked halloumi until heated through.

4. Plate the curried halloumi with the sauce, along with rice of your choice. Garnish with the coriander leaves, and serve hot.

Per Serving:
Calories: 590; Total Fat: 48.1g; Saturated Fat: 28.2g; Carbohydrates: 8.8 g; Protein: 29.2 g; Fiber: 4.8g

CAULIFLOWER STEAKS & ROMESCO SAUCE

COOK TIME: 25 MINS | MAKES: 4 SERVINGS

INGREDIENTS:

- 1 small cauliflower head, stem removed
- White pepper
- Kosher salt
- 1/2 tsp. onion powder
- 1/4 tsp. garlic powder
- extra-virgin avocado oil
- 1 medium red pepper

- 15 oz. canned chickpeas, drained and rinsed
- 1 tsp. freshly squeezed lemon juice
- 1 tsp. crushed garlic
- 1 tbsp. tomato paste
- 1/4 cup almond slivers
- 1/4 cup Greek olives, pitted and sliced
- Fresh parsley, chopped, for garnish

DIRECTIONS:

1. Cover a large baking tray with greaseproof paper, and set the oven to preheat to 450°F, with the wire rack in the center of the oven.

2. Place the head of cauliflower on a wooden chopping board, and slice 4 1-inch thick steaks. Arrange the steaks on the prepared baking tray. In a small glass bowl, whisk together 1 teaspoon pepper, 1/2 teaspoon salt, onion powder, and garlic powder. Drizzle the top of each steak with 1 teaspoon of olive oil, and season with a few sprinkles of the spice mixture. Flip the steak, and repeat the process with more olive oil and the remaining spice. Make room on the tray for the whole bell pepper, and drizzle with 1 teaspoon of oil.

3. Place the tray in the oven, and bake for 15 minutes, or until the bell pepper is nicely roasted, and the skin is brown. Remove the tray from the oven, and transfer the roasted bell pepper to a paper bag. Fold the edges over, trapping in the steam, and set aside.

4. Place the chickpeas in a medium-sized bowl, and add 1 teaspoon of oil, and a generous pinch each of salt and pepper. Toss to coat. Add the coated chickpeas to the pan, and flip the cauliflower steaks using a spatula. Return the tray to the oven for an additional 10 minutes, until the steaks are tender on the inside, and crispy on the outside.

5. Carefully remove the hot bell pepper from the bag. Slice, and remove the stem and seeds. Place the slices in a high-powered food processor, along with the lemon juice, garlic, tomato paste, almond slivers, and 1/4 teaspoon each of salt and pepper. Pulse on high until you have a smooth paste.

6. Plate the cauliflower steaks, and top with the roasted chickpeas. Drizzle with the romesco sauce, before garnishing with the olives and parsley. Serve hot.

Per Serving:
Calories: 360; Total Fat: 25g; Carbohydrates: 29g; Protein: 11g; Sodium: 904mg; Fiber: 10g

RICOTTA SALATA PASTA

COOK TIME: 15 MINS | MAKES: 4 SERVINGS

INGREDIENTS:

- 1 lb. fusilli
- 1/3 cup avocado oil
- 1/4 tsp. white pepper
- 1/2 tsp. lemon zest, finely grated
- 1 tbsp. freshly squeezed lemon juice
- 3 tsp. crushed garlic
- 2 cups fresh mint leaves, chopped (more for garnish)
- 1/4 cup almond slivers
- 1/2 cup ricotta Salata, grated (more for garnish)

DIRECTIONS:

1. Cook the fusilli in salted water, according to package instructions.

2. Meanwhile, pulse the avocado oil, pepper, zest, lemon juice, garlic, mint leaves, and almond slivers on high in a food processor, until you have a lump-free sauce. Add 1/2 cup of cheese, and pulse a few times until all of the ingredients are properly combined.

3. Once the pasta is cooked, drain through a colander set over the sink. Transfer to a serving bowl, and scrape the sauce from the food processor onto the cooked pasta. Gently stir to combine. Garnish with mint and extra cheese before serving hot.

Per Serving:
Calories: 619; Total Fat: 31g; Saturated Fat: 8g; Carbohydrates: 70g; Protein: 21g; Sodium: 113mg; Fiber: 4g

CURRIED CHICKPEA BURGERS

COOK TIME: 10-15 MINS | MAKES: 6 SERVINGS

INGREDIENTS:

- 1/4 cup fat-free red wine vinaigrette
- 1 medium shallot, thinly sliced
- 1/4 cup fresh parsley
- 1/4 cup panko breadcrumbs
- 1/3 cup lightly toasted walnuts, chopped
- 15 oz. canned chickpeas, drained and rinsed
- 1/2 tsp. white pepper
- 1 tsp. curry powder
- 1 tsp. ground turmeric
- 2 large free-range eggs
- 2 tbsp. French mustard
- 1/3 cup fat-free mayonnaise
- 6 sesame seed hamburger buns, split and toasted
- 6 romaine lettuce leaves
- 3 tbsp. fresh basil leaves, lightly chopped

DIRECTIONS:

1. Set the oven to preheat to 375°F, with the wire rack in the upper third of the oven. Lightly coat a baking tray with baking spray.

2. Place the vinaigrette in a shallow bowl, and submerge the shallot slices. Set aside.

3. Pulse the parsley, breadcrumbs, walnuts, and chickpeas on high in a food processor, until all of the ingredients are properly combined. Add the pepper, curry powder, turmeric, and eggs, before pulsing again until there are no longer any lumps.

4. Form the mixture into 6 patties of approximately the same size, and place on the prepared baking tray. Bake the patties for 10-15 minutes, or until they are cooked all the way through.

5. In a small glass bowl, whisk together the mustard and mayonnaise. Spread the mixture over the open sides of each bun.

6. Place a single lettuce leaf on one side of each bun, and top with the soaked shallots. Add one cooked patty to each bun, and garnish with the basil leaves before closing the burgers, and serving hot.

Per Serving:
Calories: 386; Total Fat: 12g; Saturated Fat: 2g; Carbohydrates: 54g; Protein: 16g; Sodium: 732 mg; Fiber: 9g

NUTTY BUTTERNUT COUSCOUS

COOK TIME: 50 MINS | MAKES: 4 SERVINGS

INGREDIENTS:

- 3 tbsp. avocado oil
- 1 medium shallot, chopped
- 1/4 tsp. cayenne pepper
- 1 tsp. kosher salt (divided)
- 1 tsp. ground cumin
- 1 tsp. ground coriander
- 1 cinnamon stick
- 6 canned plum tomatoes, crushed
- 3 tsp. crushed garlic
- 1/2 cup currants

- 1 tsp. lemon zest
- 4 1/2 cups vegetable stock (divided)
- 16 oz. canned chickpeas, drained and rinsed
- 1 1/2 lbs. butternut squash, diced
- 4 cups Swiss chard, chopped
- 1/2 lemon, juiced
- 1/4 tsp. white pepper
- 1 cup whole-wheat couscous
- 1/4 cup toasted pine nuts

DIRECTIONS:

1. In a small saucepan over medium heat, heat the oil before adding the shallots, and frying for 10 minutes, or until the shallots are nicely caramelized. Stir in the cayenne pepper, 1/2 teaspoon salt, cumin, coriander, cinnamon stick, tomatoes, and garlic. Cook for 3 minutes, until the tomatoes begin to soften. Add the currants, lemon zest, 3 cups of stock, chickpeas, and butternut. Stir until the broth gently begins to simmer.

2. Place a lid over the saucepan, leaving a small gap for the steam to escape. Simmer the butternut for about 25 minutes, stirring occasionally to prevent burning. When the butternut is soft, add the Swiss chard, and stir for 2-3 minutes, until the chard reduces in size. Add the lemon juice, and stir to combine.

3. While the butternut is still simmering, place the remaining stock, remaining salt, and white pepper in a small pot, and bring to a boil over medium heat. Once the stock begins to boil, immediately transfer the pot to a wooden chopping board, and stir in the couscous. Place a lid on the pot, and let stand for about 5 minutes, until the couscous is tender, and all of the stock has been absorbed. Use a fork to separate the couscous in the pot.

4. Divide the couscous between 4 bowls. Ladle the cooked butternut over the couscous, and garnish with the pine nuts before serving hot.

Per Serving:
Calories: 920; Total Fat: 26g; Saturated Fat: 3g; Carbohydrates: 141g; Protein: 40g; Sodium: 1,532mg; Fiber: 30g

TURKISH-STYLE GRILLED MEATBALLS

COOK TIME: 45 MINS | MAKES: 4 SERVINGS

INGREDIENTS:

- Extra-virgin olive oil
- 2 cups water
- 1 cup red lentils
- 1 tsp. kosher salt
- 1/2 cup bulgur
- 1 medium shallot, finely chopped
- 2 tbsp. tomato paste
- 1 tsp. ground cumin
- 1/2 lemon, juiced
- 3 spring onions, thinly sliced
- 1/4 cup fresh parsley, finely chopped

DIRECTIONS:

1. Set the oven to preheat to 400°F, with the wire rack in the center of the oven. Coat a large, rimmed baking tray with olive oil.

2. Place the water and lentils in a medium-sized pot, and bring to a boil over medium-high heat. Once the water begins to boil, reduce the heat to low, and simmer for about 15 minutes, stirring at regular intervals to prevent burning. When the lentils have softened, and the majority of the water has been absorbed, transfer the pot to a wooden chopping board, and stir in the salt and bulgur. Place a lid on the pot, and let the bulgur and lentils stand for 15 minutes to absorb the rest of the water.

3. While you leave the bulgur on the counter, heat 1/3 cup of olive oil in a medium-sized frying pan over medium heat. When the oil is nice and hot, add the shallots, and fry for about 5 minutes, or until the shallots become translucent. Stir in the tomato paste for an additional 2 minutes. Turn off the heat, and stir in the cumin.

4. When the bulgur has softened and absorbed all of the water, scrape the cooked shallots into the pot, and add the lemon juice, spring onions, and parsley, stirring to combine.

5. Form the mixture into bite-sized meatballs. Arrange all of the meatballs on the prepared baking tray, and coat with 2 tablespoons of olive oil. Place the tray in the oven for 15-20 minutes, until the meatballs are cooked all the way through, and nicely browned. Serve hot, with a dip of your choice.

Per Serving:
Calories: 460; Total Fat: 25g; Saturated Fat: 4g; Carbohydrates: 48g; Protein: 16g; Sodium: 604mg; Fiber: 19g

CROATIAN DOUBLE-CRUSTED VEGETABLE TART

COOK TIME: 20 MINS | MAKES: 4 SERVINGS

INGREDIENTS:

- 1 1/4 tsp. Himalayan salt
- 4 1/2 cups all-purpose flour
- 1 cup warm water
- 1 1/2 cups avocado oil (plus 3 tbsp.)
- 1/4 small green cabbage, thinly sliced
- 1 lb. spinach, ribs removed, and leaves chopped
- 1/4 tsp. white pepper
- 4 tsp. crushed garlic

DIRECTIONS:

1. Place 1 teaspoon of salt, along with the 4 1/2 cups of flour, in a medium-sized bowl, and whisk to combine. Pour the warm water and 1 1/2 cups of oil into the bowl, and stir with a fork, until the mixture just comes together. Use your hands to bring the dough together in a ball. Cover in cling wrap, and chill for 30 minutes.

2. Meanwhile, place the cabbage and spinach in a clean mixing bowl, and add 2 tablespoons of oil, and the remaining salt and pepper. Toss until all of the vegetables are evenly coated.

3. Set the oven to preheat to 400°F, with the wire rack in the center of the oven.

4. When the dough is nicely chilled. Divide into two balls, and place the balls on two pieces of lightly floured greaseproof paper. Roll the balls into 1/4-inch thick circles.

5. Spread the coated vegetables over one of the dough circles, leaving a small border around the edges. Carefully place the second round over the vegetables to create a lid. Use a fork to seal the edges like a pie. Place the double-crusted tart on a lightly sprayed baking tray, and bake in the oven for 20 minutes, or until the crust is lightly browned.

6. While the tart is baking, place 1 tablespoon of oil with the crushed garlic in a small glass bowl, and whisk to combine.

7. When the tart is done, immediately brush the top crust with the oil and garlic. Slice, and serve while still hot.

Per Serving:
Calories: 670; Total Fat: 45g; Saturated Fat: 6g; Carbohydrates: 62g; Protein: 10g; Sodium: 504mg; Fiber: 5g

CHEESY PUMPKIN & MUSHROOM LASAGNA

COOK TIME: 1 HOUR | MAKES: 6 SERVINGS

INGREDIENTS:

- 2 tbsp. extra-virgin olive oil
- 1 small shallot, chopped
- 1/2 lb. button mushrooms, sliced
- 1/2 tsp. Himalayan salt
- 1 tsp. dried sage leaves
- 1/2 cup half-and-half cream

- 15 oz. canned solid-pack pumpkin
- Freshly ground black pepper
- 9 no-cook, spinach flavored lasagna noodles
- 1 cup mozzarella cheese, grated
- 1 cup reduced-fat ricotta cheese
- 3/4 cup parmesan cheese, grated

DIRECTIONS:

1. Set the oven to preheat to 375°F, with the wire rack in the center of the oven.

2. Heat the olive oil in a small frying pan over medium heat. When the oil is nice and hot, fry the shallots and mushrooms with a 1/4 teaspoon salt, until the shallots are soft, and the mushrooms darken in color. Transfer the pan to a wooden chopping board.

3. In a medium-sized bowl, stir together the sage leaves, cream, pumpkin, remaining salt, and a large pinch of pepper.

4. Lightly coat an 11x7-inch casserole dish with baking spray. Spread 1/2 cup of the pumpkin mixture on the bottom of the dish, and top with 3 lasagna noodles. Don't worry if the noodles overlap slightly. Spread 1/2 cup of the pumpkin mixture over the noodles, followed by half of the fried mushrooms. Sprinkle the mushrooms with 1/2 cup mozzarella and 1/2 cup of ricotta in two separate layers. Sprinkle the cheese with 1/4 cup parmesan. Repeat the steps with the remaining ingredients to complete the lasagna. Reserve 1/4 cup of parmesan for later.

5. Cover the dish with tin foil, and place in the oven for 45 minutes. Remove the dish from the oven, and discard the foil. Sprinkle the remaining parmesan over the top of the lasagna before returning the dish to the oven, and baking for an additional 10-15 minutes, or until the cheese is bubbly, and nicely toasted.

6. Allow the lasagna to rest for 10 minutes on the counter before slicing, and serving hot.

Tip: You can prepare and freeze the unbaked lasagna ahead of time. To bake the frozen lasagna, partially thaw, and refrigerate overnight, before baking in the oven at 375°F until the cheese bubbles. Baking time may need to be increased – use a meat thermometer to test the temperature in the middle of the lasagna. The temperature should read 165°F when ready.

Per Serving:
Calories: 310; Total Fat: 12g; Saturated Fat: 6g; Carbohydrates: 32g; Protein: 17g; Sodium: 497 mg; Fiber: 5g

FRESH HERB & SUMMER VEGETABLE CASSEROLE

COOK TIME: 1 HOUR | MAKES: 4 SERVINGS

INGREDIENTS:

- 6 tbsp. extra-virgin olive oil (divided)
- 2 tsp. crushed garlic
- 2 medium shallots, diced
- 1 green bell pepper, seeded and thinly sliced
- 2 red bell peppers, seeded and thinly sliced
- 3 medium zucchinis, halved lengthwise, and thinly sliced into half rounds
- 2 medium eggplants, halved lengthwise, and thinly sliced into half rounds
- 1 tsp. kosher salt
- 1/2 tsp. white pepper
- 14 oz. canned diced tomatoes, drained
- 1 tbsp. fresh chives, chopped
- 1 tbsp. fresh basil, chopped
- 1 tbsp. fresh parsley, chopped
- 8 oz. panko breadcrumbs
- 6 oz. gruyere cheese, grated

DIRECTIONS:

1. Set the oven to preheat to 375°F, with the wire rack in the center of the oven. Lightly coat a large casserole dish with baking spray.

2. In a frying pan over medium heat, heat 5 tablespoons of olive oil. When the oil is nice and hot, add the garlic and shallots, frying for about 8 minutes, or until the shallots are nicely caramelized. Add the bell peppers, zucchinis, and eggplants, frying and tossing for 10 minutes, or until the vegetables are tender, but still crisp. Add in the salt, pepper, and canned tomatoes, stirring until the sauce begins to simmer. Allow the sauce to maintain a gentle simmer for 15 minutes, stirring at regular intervals to prevent burning.

3. Meanwhile, in a medium-sized mixing bowl, stir together 1 tablespoon of oil, chives, basil, parsley, and bread crumbs.

4. Scrape the contents of the pan into the prepared casserole dish, spreading it out in an even layer. Top with the gruyere, followed by the herbs and breadcrumbs. Bake in the oven until the bread crumbs are nicely toasted, and the casserole is bubbling – about 30 minutes.

5. Serve immediately.

Per Serving:
Calories: 701; Total Fat: 37g; Saturated Fat: 10g; Carbohydrates: 77g; Protein: 23g; Sodium: 1,185mg; Fiber: 18g

ITALIAN-SPICED MUSHROOM BEANBALLS

COOK TIME: 25-30 MINS | MAKES: 3 SERVINGS

INGREDIENTS:

- 2 tbsp. extra-virgin avocado oil (divided)
- 3 tsp. crushed garlic
- 8 oz. crimini mushrooms, finely chopped
- Himalayan salt
- White pepper
- 14 oz. canned turtle beans, drained, rinsed, and patted dry
- 14 oz. whole canned tomatoes, with the juices
- 3/4 tsp. Italian seasoning (divided)
- 1 tsp. parmesan cheese, shredded
- 1 tbsp. nutritional yeast
- 1 large free-range egg, lightly beaten
- 1/4 tsp. garlic salt
- Fresh parsley, chopped, for garnish

DIRECTIONS:

1. Cover a medium-sized baking tray with greaseproof paper, and set the oven to preheat to 425°F, with the wire rack in the center of the oven.

2. In a large frying pan, heat 1 tablespoon of the oil over medium heat. When the oil is nice and hot, fry the garlic and mushrooms for about 5-10 minutes, or until the mushrooms darken in color. Season to taste with salt and pepper.

3. Place the beans in a large mixing bowl, and mash using a fork or potato masher. Stir in 3 tablespoons of the tomato juice, 1/2 teaspoon Italian seasoning, 1 teaspoon parmesan, 1 tablespoon nutritional yeast, 1/4 teaspoon salt, a large pinch of pepper, and the egg. Scrape the cooked mushrooms into the bowl, and stir until all of the ingredients are properly combined.

4. Form the mixture into 9 balls of roughly the same size. Arrange the meatballs on the prepared baking tray, and coat with the remaining oil. Place the tray in the oven for 12-15 minutes, or until the meatballs are cooked through and nicely browned.

5. In the same pan used to fry the mushrooms, mash the tomatoes along with 1/4 cup of the juices. Stir in the remaining Italian seasoning and garlic salt. Season to taste with extra salt and pepper if desired. Heat over medium heat until the sauce is gently bubbling.

6. Serve the meatballs hot with the heated sauce ladled over the top, and garnished with the fresh parsley.

Per Serving:
Calories: 270; Total Fat: 11g; Carbohydrates: 31g; Protein: 14g; Sodium: 183 mg; Fiber: 11g

SPINACH & GRUYERE CANNELLONI

COOK TIME: 35 MINS | MAKES: 4 SERVINGS

INGREDIENTS:

- 1 lb. fresh spinach, stems removed, and leaves julienned
- 1/4 cup extra-virgin olive oil, plus 2 tbsp. (divided)
- 1 medium shallot, finely chopped
- 1/2 tsp. kosher salt
- 1/4 tsp. white pepper

- 1 1/4 cup panko breadcrumbs
- 1/2 cup parmesan cheese, grated (divided)
- 6 oz. gruyere cheese, grated
- 2 cups canned tomato sauce
- 1 lb. cannelloni sheets, cooked and cooled
- 1/2 cup panko breadcrumbs

DIRECTIONS:

1. Set the oven to preheat to 350°F, with the wire rack in the middle of the oven. Coat a large casserole dish with olive oil spray.

2. Fill a large pot with salted water, and bring to a boil over medium heat. Boil the spinach leaves for 3-4 minutes, or until just softened. Use tongs to transfer the cooked spinach to a bowl of ice water to cool. Allow the leaves to chill for a few minutes before transferring to a colander set over the sink, then use the back of a wooden spoon to gently press out any excess water. Place the leaves on a wooden chopping board, and chop.

3. In a medium frying pan over medium heat, heat 1/4 cup of olive oil. When the oil is nice and hot, fry the shallots for about 5minutes, or until translucent. Mix in the spinach, and simmer for 2 minutes with a lid on the pan. Scrape the spinach and shallots into a bowl, and allow to cool for 10 minutes on the counter.

4. Season the spinach and shallots with salt and pepper. Stir in the breadcrumbs, half of the parmesan, and all of the gruyere cheese.

5. Spread the canned tomato sauce over the bottom of the prepared casserole dish in an even layer.

6. Line the cannelloni sheets up on a clean work surface. Divide the spinach mixture evenly amongst the sheets. Carefully roll up the pasta sheets into 3-inch thick cylinders. Slice the cylinders into 4-inch lengths. Arrange the sliced cylinders in a single layer in the tomato sauce, cut side down. Use a basting brush to coat the tops of the cylinders with the remaining olive oil.

7. Place the breadcrumbs in a mixing bowl, and whisk in the remaining parmesan cheese. Sprinkle the mixture in an even layer over the cannelloni cylinders.

8. Place the casserole dish in the oven for about 20 minutes, or until the cylinders are nicely browned on top, and piping hot. Serve immediately.

Per Serving:
Calories: 727; Total Fat: 35g; Saturated Fat: 15g; Carbohydrates: 76g; Protein: 34g; Sodium: 1,755mg; Fiber: 12g

CRISPY VEGETABLE PIZZA

COOK TIME: 10-15 MINS | MAKES: 6 SERVINGS

INGREDIENTS:

- 1 yellow summer squash, sliced lengthwise into 1/2-inch slices
- 1 small zucchini, sliced lengthwise into 1/2-inch slices
- 1 large red sweet pepper, stemmed, seeded, and sliced
- 1 medium shallot, thinly sliced
- 2 tbsp. garlic-infused olive oil
- 1/2 tsp. Himalayan salt
- 1/4 tsp. white pepper
- 1 prebaked, 12-inch, thin whole wheat pizza crust
- 3 tbsp. jarred roasted minced garlic
- 2 cups shredded part-skim mozzarella cheese
- 1/3 cup torn fresh basil, chopped

DIRECTIONS:

1. Place all of the vegetables in a large bowl, and toss with the oil, salt, and pepper, until all of the vegetables are evenly coated.

2. Heat a large grill pan over medium heat, and grill the vegetables covered for 5 minutes, turning them halfway through.

3. Place the pizza crust on a chopping board, and spread the garlic over the crust in an even layer. Top with the roasted vegetables, and sprinkle with the cheese.

4. Place the pizza in a heated grill pan over medium heat, and grill covered for 5-7 minutes, or until the cheese is bubbling, and the base is crispy.

5. Garnish with the basil leaves before slicing, and serve hot.

Per Serving:
Calories: 324; Total Fat: 15g; Saturated Fat: 6g; Carbohydrates: 30g; Protein: 16g; Sodium: 704 mg; Fiber: 5g

SOUPS & STEWS

LENTIL & CARROT COMFORT SOUP

COOK TIME: 15-20 MINS | MAKES: 4-6 SERVINGS

INGREDIENTS:

- 2 tbsp. extra-virgin avocado oil (extra for garnish)
- 1 tsp. crushed garlic
- 1 cup shallots, chopped
- 1 medium carrot, thinly sliced
- 1/4 tsp. dried oregano
- 1/2 tsp. sweet smoked paprika
- 1/2 tsp. ground cumin
- 4 cups vegetable stock
- 1 cup lentils, thoroughly rinsed and drained
- 4 lemon slices
- Himalayan salt
- White pepper

DIRECTIONS:

1. Heat the oil in a large pot over medium heat. When the oil is nice and hot, add the garlic, shallots, and carrots. Lower the heat, and fry for about 5 minutes, or until the carrots begin to soften. Stir in the oregano, paprika, and cumin for 30 seconds.

2. Stir in the stock and lentils. Place a lid on the pot, leaving a small gap for the steam to escape. Allow the soup to simmer for 15 minutes, stirring occasionally until the lentils soften. When the lentils are cooked, turn off the stove, and stir in the lemon slices. Taste the soup, and add extra salt and a dash of pepper to taste, if needed.

3. Scoop the soup into bowls, and garnish with a few drops of oil, if desired. Serve hot.

Per Serving:
Calories: 287; Total Fat: 7g; Carbohydrates: 40g; Protein: 14g; Sodium: 576 mg; Fiber: 15g

WHITE WINE BOUILLABAISSE SOUP

COOK TIME: 1 HOUR | MAKES: 4 SERVINGS

INGREDIENTS:

- 1 lb. in-shell medium-large shrimp, thawed
- 1 tbsp. garlic-infused avocado oil (extra for drizzling)
- 1 tsp. crushed garlic
- 1/2 tsp. cayenne pepper
- 1/2 cup dry white wine
- 1/4 cup parsley, chopped (plus 2 whole stems)
- 1 whole bay leaf
- 1/4 tsp. dried thyme
- 8 oz. bottled clam juice
- 1/4 tsp. flaky sea salt
- 14.5 oz. canned diced tomatoes
- 2 cups chicken bone stock
- 1/2 lb. tilapia, sliced into 2-inch pieces
- 1/2 lemon, juiced

DIRECTIONS:

1. Remove the shrimp from their shells, and place in a bowl, reserving the shells and tails. Heat the oil in a large pot over medium heat, and add the shells, tails, garlic, and cayenne pepper. Fry for about 5 minutes, until the flavors meld.

2. Stir in the white wine, and simmer for 2 minutes, until half of the wine has cooked away. Add 2 parsley stems, the bay leaf, thyme, and clam juice, stirring until the soup reaches a gentle simmer. Simmer for 15-30 minutes, lowering the heat as needed, to maintain a gentle simmer until the soup thickens. Use a slotted spoon to remove all the solid ingredients, including shells, tails, parsley, and bay leaf.

3. Stir in the salt, tomatoes, and chicken stock, bringing the soup back up to a gentle simmer. Stir in the shrimp and tilapia, making sure that all of the seafood is covered in the soup. Set a timer for 3 minutes, and simmer the soup with a lid on the pot. Keep an eye on the temperature to maintain a simmer. The fish is cooked when completely solid. Transfer the pot to a wooden chopping board, and stir in the lemon juice.

4. Spoon the soup into bowls, and serve hot, garnished with chopped parsley and a few drizzles of oil.

Per Serving:
Calories: 158; Total Fat: 6g; Carbohydrates: 7g; Protein: 29g; Sodium: 850 mg; Fiber: 1g

ITALIAN BEAN & CABBAGE SOUP

COOK TIME: 6-8 HOURS | MAKES: 8 SERVINGS

INGREDIENTS:

- 4 cups chicken broth
- 6 oz. canned tomato paste
- 1/2 tsp. Himalayan salt
- 1 whole bay leaf
- 2 fresh thyme sprigs
- 2 tsp. crushed garlic
- 15.5 oz. white beans, drained and rinsed
- 1 small shallot, chopped
- 2 large carrots, chopped
- 4 celery stalks, chopped
- 1 1/2 lbs. cabbage, shredded
- Parmesan cheese, grated, for garnish

DIRECTIONS:

1. In a large slow cooker, whisk together the chicken broth and tomato paste, until properly combined. Stir in the salt, bay leaf, thyme sprigs, garlic, beans, shallots, carrots, celery, and cabbage, until all of the ingredients are properly combined. Place the lid on the slow cooker, and cook on low for 6-8 hours, until the vegetables are fork-tender.

2. Discard the bay leaf and thyme sprigs. Spoon the soup into bowls, and serve hot, garnished with parmesan.

Per Serving:
Calories: 111; Total Fat: 0g; Saturated Fat: 0g; Carbohydrates: 21g; Protein: 8g; Sodium: 537 mg; Fiber: 6g

ONE-POT MOROCCAN LENTIL STEW

COOK TIME: 30 MINS | MAKES: 4 SERVINGS

INGREDIENTS:

- 2 tbsp. extra-virgin avocado oil
- 1 tbsp. curry powder
- 1 tsp. ground turmeric
- 1 tsp. ground cumin
- 1 tsp. Himalayan salt
- 1 large shallot, diced
- 4 tsp. crushed garlic
- 2 tbsp. fresh ginger, minced
- 1 red bell pepper, seeded and diced
- 1 lb. cubed pumpkin
- 6 cups vegetable stock
- 1 1/2 cups red lentils, rinsed and drained
- 1/4 cup fresh coriander leaves, chopped, for garnish

DIRECTIONS:

1. In a large pot over medium heat, heat the oil before adding the curry powder, turmeric, and cumin. Stir for 1 minute, allowing the flavors to meld. Stir in the salt and shallots, frying for 5 minutes, until the shallots become translucent. Stir in the garlic and ginger for an additional 2 minutes. Add the peppers and pumpkin cubes to the pot, stirring to combine. Finally, add in the stock and lentils, and stir until the stew begins to bubble.

2. Lower the heat to maintain a gentle simmer, and cook with the lid off the pot for 20 minutes, stirring occasionally, until the lentils have softened.

3. Ladle the soup into bowls, and serve hot, garnished with chopped coriander leaves.

Per Serving:
Calories: 458; Total Fat: 11g; Saturated Fat: 2g; Carbohydrates: 64g; Protein: 29g; Sodium: 1,743mg; Fiber: 28g

SLOW-COOKED VENISON STEW

COOK TIME: 3-4 HOURS | MAKES: 6-8 SERVINGS

INGREDIENTS:

- 3 whole bay leaves
- 4 whole cloves
- 1 tsp. freshly ground black pepper
- 4 fresh thyme sprigs
- 4 fresh parsley sprigs
- 1/4 cup extra-virgin olive oil (plus 2 tbsp.)
- 2 lbs. venison, cut into 2-inch cubes
- 1 small shallot, diced

- 3 tsp. crushed garlic
- 1/2 tsp. white pepper
- 1 tsp. kosher salt
- 1 tsp. ground turmeric powder
- 1 tbsp. tomato paste
- 3 cups dry red wine
- 12 oz. button mushrooms, sliced
- Cooked rice for serving

DIRECTIONS:

1. Place the bay leaves, cloves, black pepper, thyme, and parsley in the center of a small, clean cheesecloth. Fold up the edges, and secure the bundle using butchers twine. Set aside.

2. Heat 2 tablespoons of olive oil in a large, cast-iron pot over medium-high heat. When the oil is nice and hot fry the venison cubes for about 5 minutes, until nicely browned on all sides. You may fry the venison cubes in batches, to avoid over-crowding the pot. Transfer the browned venison to a bowl, and tent with foil to keep warm.

3. Add the diced shallot to the pot, and fry for 5 minutes, until the shallots become translucent. Stir in the garlic for 1 additional minute. Stir in the browned venison. Season the venison with the salt and pepper. Whisk in the turmeric, tomato paste and wine. Bring the mixture to a boil while stirring, dislodging any food that stuck to the bottom of the pot. Stir in the mushrooms and the spice bundle.

4. Simmer the stew for 3-3 1/2 hours over low heat, stirring occasionally. Remove the pot from the heat when the venison is falling apart.

5. Transfer the cooked venison to a separate bowl, and tent to keep warm. Discard the spice bundle. Use a handheld blender to puree the remaining contents of the stew. Stir in the 1/4 cup of olive oil before returning the pot to heat, and stirring for a few minutes until the stew thickens. Stir in the venison.

6. Serve the stew hot, over rice of your choice.

Per Serving:
Calories: 462; Total Fat: 22.6g; Saturated Fat: 3.3g; Carbohydrates: 6.1g; Protein: 34.5g; Fiber: 1.1g

CHICKEN & CHARD WILD RICE SOUP

COOK TIME: 5 1/2 HOURS | MAKES: 6 SERVINGS

INGREDIENTS:

- 1/4 tsp. kosher salt
- 1/2 tsp. freshly ground black pepper
- 1/2 tsp. dried thyme
- 1 tsp. crushed garlic
- 2/3 cup raw wild rice
- 10 oz. canned reduced-fat, low-sodium, condensed cream of chicken soup, undiluted
- 14.5 oz. low-sodium canned chicken stock
- 3 cups warm water
- 2 cups Swiss chard, stems removed, chopped
- 3 cups cooked, cubed chicken breast

DIRECTIONS:

1. In a large slow cooker, stir together the salt, pepper, thyme, garlic, rice, chicken soup, chicken stock, and water. Cook the soup on low for 5-7 hours, or until the rice has softened.

2. Add the chard and chicken to the pot, stirring to combine. Cook for an additional 15 minutes, or until the chard has wilted. The chicken should be heated through at this stage.

3. Ladle the soup into bowls, and serve hot.

Per Serving:
Calories: 212; Total Fat: 3g; Saturated Fat: 2g; Carbohydrates: 19g; Protein: 25g; Sodium: 523mg; Fiber: 2g

BEEFY YAM STEW

COOK TIME: 20 MINS | MAKES: 4 SERVINGS

INGREDIENTS:

- 28 oz. canned low-sodium beef stock
- 3/4 lbs. lean ground beef
- 1/3 tsp. red pepper flakes
- 1/2 tsp. dried thyme
- 1 tsp. crushed garlic
- 1 tbsp. currents
- 1/2 cup V8 juice
- 1 small shallot, finely chopped
- 2 medium yams, peeled and cubed (1/2-inch cubes)

DIRECTIONS:

1. Bring the beef stock to a rolling boil in a large pot over medium-high heat. Stir in the ground beef. Place a lid on the pot, and cook for 3 minutes, stirring at regular intervals to prevent burning.

2. Remove the lid, and stir in the red pepper flakes, thyme, garlic, currents, V8 juice, shallots, and yams. Stir the stew for a few minutes until the sauce begins to boil again. Once the sauce is boiling, lower the heat to maintain a gentle simmer. Allow the stew to simmer for 15 minutes, stirring occasionally, until the ground beef is cooked all the way through, and the yams are fork-tender.

3. Ladle the soup into bowls, and serve hot.

Per Serving:
Calories: 265; Total Fat: 7g; Saturated Fat: 3g; Carbohydrates: 29g; Protein: 20g; Sodium: 532 mg; Fiber: 4g

GREAT NORTHERN BEAN SOUP

COOK TIME: 20 MINS | MAKES: 5 SERVINGS

INGREDIENTS:

- 2 tbsp. extra-virgin olive oil
- 1 tsp. crushed garlic
- 1/2 medium shallot, diced
- 1 celery stalk, diced
- 1 medium carrot, diced
- 1/2 tsp. kosher salt
- White pepper
- 4 cups spinach, chopped
- 1 tsp. Italian seasoning
- 14.5 oz. canned diced tomatoes
- 3 cups vegetable stock
- 15 oz. canned great northern beans, drained and rinsed
- 1 tsp. red wine vinegar

DIRECTIONS:

1. Heat 2 tablespoons of olive oil in a large pot over medium heat. When the oil is nice and hot, add the garlic, shallots, celery, carrots, 1/4 teaspoon salt, and a generous pinch of white pepper. Fry the vegetables for 5 minutes before stirring in the spinach. Fry for an additional 5 minutes, or until all of the vegetables have softened.

2. Stir in the Italian seasoning, the remaining salt, and an extra dash of pepper. Add the canned tomatoes with their juices, the vegetable stock, and the great northern beans. Allow the soup to simmer for 10 minutes, stirring at regular intervals while keeping an eye on the temperature. Add the red wine vinegar, and stir.

3. Spoon the soup into bowls, and serve hot.

Per Serving:
Calories: 182; Total Fat: 7g; Carbohydrates: 26g; Protein: 7g; Sodium: 892 mg; Fiber; 8g

CHEESY SALMON & VEGETABLE SOUP

COOK TIME: 20 MINS | MAKES: 2 SERVINGS

INGREDIENTS:

- 1 cup low-sodium chicken stock
- 1 1/2 cups warm water
- 1 large carrot, thinly sliced (1/2-inch thick slices)
- 1 large russet potato, cut into 1 1/2-inch thick pieces
- 1 cup button mushrooms, thinly sliced
- 1/4 cup low-fat evaporated milk
- 1 tbsp. all-purpose flour
- 1/4 cup strong cheddar cheese, grated
- 1/2 lb. wild salmon fillets, cut into 1 1/2-inch pieces
- 1/8 tsp. kosher salt
- 1/4 tsp. white pepper
- 1 tbsp. fresh dill, chopped

DIRECTIONS:

1. In a large pot over medium-high heat, whisk together the chicken stock, water, carrots, and potato. Bring the soup to a boil while stirring. Once the soup begins to boil, lower the heat to medium, and simmer for 10-15 minutes, or until the vegetables are tender. Stir at regular intervals to prevent burning. Add in the mushrooms.

2. In a small glass bowl, whisk together the evaporated milk and flour to form a lump-free paste. Whisk the paste into the soup, and bring the soup back up to a boil while stirring. Bring the soup back down to a simmer over a lower heat, and stir in the cheese, until properly incorporated into the soup.

3. With the heat on medium-low, stir in the salmon, and cook for 3-4 minutes, until the fish is completely opaque and flaky. Remove the pot from the heat, and stir in the salt and pepper.

4. Ladle the soup into bowls, and garnish with the fresh dill before serving hot.

Per Serving:
Calories: 398; Total Fat: 14g; Saturated Fat: 4g; Carbohydrates: 37g; Protein: 30g; Sodium: 647 mg; Fiber: 3g

DELICIOUS CHICKPEA & PASTA SOUP

COOK TIME: 15 MINS | MAKES: 4 SERVINGS

INGREDIENTS:

- 15 oz. canned chickpeas, drained and rinsed
- 4 cups chicken stock
- pinch of saffron
- 1 tsp. kosher salt
- 1/3 cup avocado oil
- 6 oz. farfalle pasta, cooked according to package instructions, and thoroughly drained

DIRECTIONS:

1. Bring the chickpeas and stock to a boil in a large pot over medium-high heat. Lower the heat, and simmer for 10 minutes until the chickpeas have softened, stirring at regular intervals to prevent burning. Add the saffron and salt, stirring to incorporate.

2. While the soup simmers, add the avocado oil to a large frying pan, and heat over medium-high heat. Once the cooked pasta has stood in the colander for a while and is very dry, add 1/3 of the pasta to the hot oil, and fry for about 3 minutes, or until the edges are nice and crispy. Use a slotted spoon to transfer the crisped pasta to a paper towel-lined plate. Reserve the oil for serving.

3. Stir the remaining cooked pasta into the pot of soup.

4. Ladle the soup into bowls, and garnish with the crispy pasta, and a few drops of the reserved oil from the frying pan. Serve hot, and enjoy!

Per Serving:
Calories: 690; Total Fat: 25g; Saturated Fat: 4g; Carbohydrates: 89g; Protein: 30g; Sodium: 1,381 mg; Fiber: 19g

SPICY PORK & BEAN STEW

COOK TIME: 3 HOURS | MAKES: 6 SERVINGS

INGREDIENTS:

- 2 tbsp. extra-virgin olive oil
- 1 lb. pork shoulder, cut into large chunks
- 1 medium shallot, diced
- 1 tsp. kosher salt
- 2 whole bay leaves
- 1 1/2 tsp. ground cilantro
- 1 small ham hock

- 1 lb. canned great northern beans, drained and rinsed
- 1/4 cup canned crushed tomatoes
- 1 1/2 tsp. chili paste
- 6 whole garlic cloves, peeled
- 1 large carrot, cut into rounds
- 1 lb. Portuguese Linguiça sausage, left whole
- 1/4 cup fresh parsley, chopped

DIRECTIONS:

1. Set the oven to preheat to 300°F, with the wire rack in the center of the oven.

2. Heat the olive oil in a large, oven-safe pot, over medium-high heat. When the oil is nice and hot, fry the pork for a few minutes per side, until it is evenly browned. Transfer the browned pork to a bowl and set aside.

3. Fry the shallots in the same pot for about 5 minutes, or until they become translucent. Scrape the cooked pork back into the pot, and stir in the salt, bay leaves, cilantro, and ham hock. Add the beans and tomatoes, and stir to combine.

4. Add enough water to the pot to submerge the pork up to about 1-inch. Stir while bringing the water to a boil. Once the water begins to boil, cover the pot. Place the pot in the oven until the beans have softened – about 90 minutes.

5. Stir in the chili paste, garlic, carrots, and sausage. Cover the pot again, and bake in the oven until the carrots are fork-tender – about 30 more minutes.

6. Remove the pot from the oven. Take out the sausage, and carefully slice it into semi-thick rounds, then stir them back into the stew. Cover the stew, and bake in the oven for a final 10 minutes.

7. Place the pot on a wooden chopping board, and allow the stew to cool for 10 minutes before scooping into bowls, and garnishing with the parsley. Serve immediately.

Per Serving:
Calories: 813; Total Fat: 44g; Saturated Fat: 14g; Carbohydrates: 52g; Protein: 52g; Sodium: 1,036 mg; Fiber: 13g

CHEESY TOMATO & ONION SOUP

COOK TIME: 1-2 HOURS | MAKES: 6 SERVINGS

INGREDIENTS:

- 1/2 cup extra-virgin avocado oil
- 2 large yellow onions, halved and thinly sliced, crosswise
- 1 tsp. kosher salt
- 2 tsp. crushed garlic
- 4 cups warm water
- 28 oz. canned San Marzano tomatoes
- 6 slices crusty French bread
- 6 thin slices provolone cheese
- 1/3 cup parmesan cheese, grated

DIRECTIONS:

1. In a large pot over medium heat, heat the oil before adding the onions, salt, and garlic. Fry the onions and garlic for about 15 minutes, or until the onions are properly caramelized and fork-tender.

2. Pour the water and tomatoes into the pot, and bring to a boil while stirring. Once the soup is boiling, lower the heat to maintain a gentle simmer. Place a lid on the pot, and simmer for 45 minutes, stirring occasionally to prevent burning. Remove the lid after 45 minutes, and simmer for an additional 15 minutes with the lid off the pot, or until the soup thickens.

3. When the soup is ready, toast the crusty bread until golden. Place one slice of toasted bread at the bottom of each bowl, and top with 1 slice of provolone. Stir the soup to get an even distribution of onions, before ladling it into the bowls on top of the bread and cheese.

4. Garnish the soup with parmesan, and serve hot. Enjoy the delicious cheesy flavors!

Per Serving:
Calories: 364; Total Fat: 26g; Saturated Fat: 7g; Carbohydrates: 22g; Protein: 13g; Sodium: 1,640 mg; Fiber: 5g

POTATO & LEEK SOUP

COOK TIME: 25 MINS | MAKES: 4 SERVINGS

INGREDIENTS:

- 8 cups vegetable stock
- 3/4 tsp. Himalayan salt (divided)
- 1 tsp. freshly ground black pepper
- 1 medium leek, sliced into thick rounds
- 1 lb. carrots, peeled and diced
- 1 lb. russet potatoes, peeled and diced
- 1 lb. turnips, peeled and cubed (1-inch cubes)
- 1 red bell pepper, sliced into strips
- 1 lb. haricot verts
- 5 whole garlic cloves
- 2/3 cup avocado oil
- 1 tsp. freshly squeezed lemon juice
- 2 tbsp. fresh coriander leaves, chopped

DIRECTIONS:

1. In a large pot over medium-high heat, bring the stock, salt, and pepper to a rolling boil. Once the water is boiling, add the leeks. Wait for the stock to begin boiling again before stirring in the carrots. Wait for the water to boil again after adding each vegetable, and stirring. Once you have added the bell pepper strips, let the soup boil for 3 minutes, and then add the haricot verts.

2. While the soup is boiling, place the garlic and remaining salt in a food processor, and pulse on high until fine. Scrape the crushed garlic into a medium-sized bowl, and gradually whisk in the avocado oil. Whisk until the mixture becomes very thick before adding the lemon juice. Whisk to combine.

3. Ladle the soup into bowls, and top with a dollop of the garlic sauce. Top the sauce with the fresh coriander leaves, and serve immediately.

Per Serving:
Calories: 559; Total Fat: 37g; Saturated Fat: 6g; Carbohydrates: 46g; Protein: 15g; Sodium: 2,130 mg; Fiber: 10g

RED WINE BRAISED BEEF STEW

COOK TIME: 45 MINS | MAKES: 4 SERVINGS

INGREDIENTS:

- 1 tbsp. extra-virgin avocado oil
- 1 lb. beef stew meat, cut into bite-sized pieces
- 8 oz. button mushrooms, diced
- 3 tbsp. tomato paste
- 1/2 cup dry red wine
- 3 1/2 cups beef stock (divided)
- 1 tsp. Italian seasoning
- 2 tsp. crushed garlic
- 1 medium carrot, sliced into half-moons
- 1/2 medium shallot, diced
- 2 medium russet potatoes, diced
- 1/4 tsp. kosher salt
- White pepper
- 1 tsp. arrowroot
- Fresh chives, chopped

DIRECTIONS:

1. In a large pot over medium-high heat, heat the oil. When the oil is nice and hot, scrape the beef cubes into it, and fry for about 5 minutes, or until the cubes are nicely browned on all sides. Add the mushrooms, and fry for an additional 5 minutes until the mushrooms darken in color. Stir in the tomato paste for 1 minute. Add the wine to the pot, and bring to a gentle boil, scraping up any bits of food that may have stuck to the bottom of the pot. When the wine has reduced by half, add 3 1/4 cups of the beef stock to the pot, stirring to combine.

2. Stir in the Italian seasoning, garlic, carrots, shallots, potatoes, salt, and a generous pinch of pepper. Allow the stew to gently simmer for about 25 minutes, or until the vegetables are fork-tender, stirring occasionally.

3. In a medium-sized bowl, whisk the arrowroot with the remaining beef stock, until dissolved. Whisk the mixture into the stew, and simmer for an additional 5 minutes.

4. Ladle the stew into bowls, and serve hot, garnished with the fresh chives.

Per Serving:
Calories: 270; Total Fat: 8g; Carbohydrates: 20g; Protein: 25g; Sodium: 713 mg; Fiber: 3g

MINTY ROSEMARY & LAMB SOUP

COOK TIME: 6 HOURS | MAKES: 6 SERVINGS

INGREDIENTS:

- 1 tbsp. extra-virgin olive oil
- 2 lbs. ground lamb
- 1 1/2 tsp. kosher salt
- 1/2 tsp. white pepper
- 1 tbsp. dried rosemary, crushed
- 1 tbsp. dried marjoram
- 3 tbsp. fresh mint leaves, chopped
- 6 tsp. crushed garlic
- 1/4 cup red wine
- 1 medium shallot, chopped
- 14.5 oz. canned diced tomatoes
- 5 cups warm water
- Greek yogurt
- Feta cheese, crumbled

DIRECTIONS:

1. Heat the oil in a large frying pan over medium-high heat. When the oil is nice and hot, fry the ground lamb for 8-10 minutes, or until it is cooked all the way through, and all the pieces have broken apart.

2. Scrape the cooked lamb into a large slow cooker. Stir in the salt, pepper, rosemary, marjoram, mint, garlic, red wine, shallots, tomatoes with juice, and water.

3. Cook the soup on low for 6-8 hours with the lid on the cooker, or until the lamb is completely tender.

4. Ladle the soup into bowls, and serve hot with a dollop of yogurt, and garnished with feta cheese.

Tip: Any leftover soup can be frozen in an airtight container. To reheat, allow the soup to partially thaw, and chill overnight before reheating in a saucepan while stirring, over medium heat.

Per Serving:
Calories: 329; Total Fat: 20g; Saturated Fat: 8g; Carbohydrates: 7g; Protein: 27g; Sodium: 784 mg; Fiber: 2g

DESSERTS

HOMEMADE FROZEN GREEK YOGURT

COOK TIME: 0 MINS | MAKES: 2 SERVINGS

INGREDIENTS:

- 3 cups low-fat plain Greek yogurt
- 1 1/2 tsp. pure vanilla essence
- 3/4 cup fine white sugar
- 1 tbsp. freshly squeezed lemon juice
- 1 tbsp. cold water
- 1 tsp. unflavored gelatin

DIRECTIONS:

1. Spoon the yogurt into a large coffee filter placed inside of a colander or sieve. Place the colander or sieve with the yogurt over a bowl, and chill covered for 2-4 hours.

2. Once the yogurt is nicely chilled, scrape the contents of the filter into a clean bowl, and throw away the strained liquid. Whisk the vanilla and sugar into the strained yogurt, until all of the sugar granules have disappeared.

3. In a small glass bowl, whisk together the cold water and lemon juice. Gently strew the gelatin over the water, and set aside to bloom on the counter for 1 minute. Place the bowl in the microwave on high for 30 seconds, before whisking with a fork. Let stand again for 1 minute, or until the gelatin is completely incorporated. Cool for a few minutes before whisking the gelatin mixture into the yogurt. Cover the bowl, and chill for 40 minutes.

4. Scrape the chilled yogurt into a store-bought ice cream freezer, and follow the package instructions to freeze the yogurt.

5. Scrape the yogurt into an airtight container, and freeze for a few hours until firm enough to scoop. Enjoy!

Per Serving:
Calories: 225; Total Fat: 3g; Saturated Fat: 2g; Carbohydrates: 36g; Protein: 4g; Sodium: 57 mg

PISTACHIO & HONEY BAKLAVA

COOK TIME: 1 HOUR 15 MINS | MAKES: 24 SERVINGS

INGREDIENTS:

- Fine zest of 1/2 lemon
- 3/4 cup water
- 1 cup raw wild honey
- 16 oz. frozen phyllo sheets, thawed
- 1 tsp. ground cinnamon

- 1/4 tsp. ground nutmeg
- 1/3 tsp. ground ginger
- 2 cups lightly toasted, chopped walnuts
- 2 cups chopped pistachios
- 1/2 lb. unsalted butter, melted

DIRECTIONS:

1. Set the oven to preheat to 325°F, with the wire rack in the center of the oven. Butter a large, rimmed baking dish.

2. In a small pot over medium-high heat, whisk together the lemon zest, water, and honey. Bring the mixture to a gentle boil while whisking. Lower the heat to maintain a gentle simmer, and simmer for 25 minutes, stirring at regular intervals, and keeping an eye on the heat to prevent burning. Transfer the pot to a potholder, and allow the mixture to cool on the counter while you prepare the rest of the dish.

3. Slice 40 phyllo sheets to fit the size of your buttered baking dish.

4. Combine the cinnamon, nutmeg, ginger, walnuts, and pistachios in a medium-sized bowl.

5. Place one sheet of phyllo in the prepared baking dish, and use a basting brush to coat the sheet with melted butter. Repeat the process until you have ten layers of buttered phyllo sheets in your dish. Strew 3/4 cup of the spiced nuts over the top buttered sheets in an even layer.

6. Add 5 more layers of buttered sheets on top of the nuts, and sprinkle with 3/4 cup of the spiced nuts. Repeat the 5 layers and 3/4 cup process until there are 4 layers. Finally, end the layers with 10 sheets of buttered phyllo pastry.

7. Use a very sharp knife to slice the pastry layers into strips of 1 1/2 x 13-inches. Slice each strip into a rectangle, from corner to corner diagonally.

8. Place the baking dish in the oven for 1 hour and 15 minutes. The pastry should be a crispy golden brown.

9. Ladle the honey mixture over the piping hot baklava, and allow it to cool completely on the counter.

10. Serve when cooled.

Per Serving:
Calories: 291; Total Fat: 20g; Saturated Fat: 6g; Carbohydrates: 26g; Protein: 6g; Sodium: 147 mg; Fiber: 2g

NUTTY-TOPPED PEAR CRISP

COOK TIME: 35 MINS | MAKES: 12 SERVINGS

INGREDIENTS:

- 1/2 tsp. ground cinnamon
- 1/2 tsp. ground ginger
- 1/2 tsp. ground coriander
- 1/3 tsp. ground nutmeg
- Pinch of salt
- Pinch of freshly ground black pepper
- 1 tsp. ground arrowroot
- 1 tsp. freshly squeezed lemon juice
- 2 tbsp. cold butter, cubed
- 1/4 cup raisins
- 6 small pears, halved, cored, and sliced (1/4-inch thick slices)
- 1 tsp. chia seeds
- 1/2 cup chopped walnuts
- 1/2 cup sliced almonds

DIRECTIONS:

1. Set the oven to preheat to 350°F, with the wire rack in the center of the oven. Coat a large baking dish with baking spray.

2. In a large bowl, stir together the cinnamon, ginger, coriander, nutmeg, salt, pepper, arrowroot, lemon juice, butter, raisins, and pears, until all of the ingredients are properly combined. Scrape the mixture into the prepared baking dish, and spread it out in an even layer.

3. In a clean bowl, stir together the chia seeds, walnuts, and almonds. Strew the mixture over the top of the pears in a single layer.

4. Place the baking dish in the oven for 35 minutes, or until the top of the crisp is golden, and the pears are crispy around the edges.

5. Let the crisp rest on the counter for 10 minutes, before serving warm with a topping of your choice, such as vanilla ice cream.

Per Serving:
Calories: 107; Total fat: 7g; Carbohydrates: 10g; Protein: 2g; Sodium: 13 mg; Fiber: 3g

TRADITIONAL VANILLA SPANISH CREAM

COOK TIME: 10 MINS | MAKES: 6 SERVINGS

INGREDIENTS:

- 1 1/4 cups unsweetened almond milk (divided)
- 1 tbsp. unflavored gelatin powder
- 1 1/4 cups full-fat heavy whipping cream
- Yolks of 3 large eggs
- 1 tsp. ground cinnamon
- 1/3 tsp. ground nutmeg
- 1 tbsp. pure vanilla essence
- Whites of 3 large eggs
- 1/2 oz. white chocolate, grated
- Low-carb sweetener to taste (optional)

DIRECTIONS:

1. Pour 1/2 cup almond milk into a glass bowl, and strew the gelatin over the top. Set the bowl aside to bloom on the counter while you prepare the rest of the dish.

2. In a medium-sized glass bowl, whisk together the remaining almond milk, whipping cream, and egg yolks. Place the bowl over a pot of boiling water – the water should not be in contact with the bottom of the bowl. Gently whisk the mixture over the boiling water until smooth, thick, and creamy.

3. Remove the glass bowl from the heat, and gently stir in the cinnamon, nutmeg, and vanilla. Cover the bowl with plastic wrap. Use your hand to gently press the plastic onto the surface of the cream. Place the covered bowl in the refrigerator for 30 minutes to chill. The cream will firm up during this time.

4. In a medium-sized bowl, whisk the egg whites to form stiff peaks. Gently fold the egg whites into the chilled cream, until properly combined. Spoon the cream into glass serving bowls or a dessert mold, and chill for 3-4 hours until the cream is completely set.

5. Garnish the set cream with the white chocolate before serving, and sprinkle with sweetener if desired.

Per Serving:
Calories: 245; Total Fat: 23.2g; Saturated Fat: 13.6g; Carbohydrates: 2.1g; Protein: 6.3g; Fiber: 0.5g

HONEY-DRIZZLED POLENTA CAKE

COOK TIME: 30 MINS | MAKES: 12 SERVINGS

INGREDIENTS:

- 1 tsp. kosher salt
- 1/3 tsp. ground nutmeg
- 1/2 tsp. ground cinnamon
- 2 tbsp. baking powder
- 1 cup raw finely ground polenta
- 2 1/2 cups all-purpose flour
- 2 large free-range eggs, lightly beaten
- 3/4 cup raw wild honey (extra for drizzling)
- 1 3/4 cups full-cream milk
- 1 cup unsalted butter, melted

DIRECTIONS:

1. Set the oven to preheat to 325°F, with the wire rack in the center of the oven. Lightly coat a large baking dish with cooking spray.

2. In a large bowl, whisk together the salt, nutmeg, cinnamon, baking powder, polenta, and flour.

3. In a separate bowl, whisk together the eggs, honey, cream, and butter, until properly combined. Add the eggs mixture to the bowl of flour and beat until you have a lump-free batter.

4. Scrape the batter into the prepared baking dish, and bake in the oven until an inserted skewer comes out clean – about 25-30 minutes.

5. Turn the cake out onto a wire rack. Once the cake is completely cool, drizzle with extra honey, and serve.

Per Serving:
Calories: 372; Total Fat: 17g; Saturated Fat: 10g; Carbohydrates: 51g; Protein: 6g; Sodium: 334 mg; Fiber: 1g

PEACH COBBLER WITH A TWIST

COOK TIME: 35-40 MINS | MAKES: 8 SERVINGS

INGREDIENTS:

- 1/2 tsp. finely grated lime zest
- 2 tsp. ground cinnamon
- 4 tsp. corn flour
- 2 tbsp. minced crystallized ginger
- 3 tbsp. fine white sugar
- 1 tbsp. freshly squeezed lime juice
- 8 medium peaches, peeled and sliced
- 1/4 cup dark brown packed sugar (plus 2 tbsp.)

- 3 tbsp. unsalted butter, softened
- 1 cup all-purpose flour
- 1/4 tsp. kosher salt
- 1/2 tsp. baking powder
- 2 tbsp. cold water
- 1/4 cup chopped pecans
- 2 tbsp. buttermilk
- Yolk of 1 large egg

DIRECTIONS:

1. Set the oven to preheat to 375°F, with the wire rack in the center of the oven. Lightly coat a large casserole dish with baking spray.

2. In a large mixing bowl, whisk together the lime zest, cinnamon, corn flour, crystallized ginger, and sugar. Stir in the lime juice and sliced peaches until all of the ingredients are properly combined. Scrape the mixture into the prepared casserole dish in an even layer.

3. In a clean mixing bowl, whisk the 1/4 cup dark brown sugar and butter together, until light and fluffy. In a separate bowl, whisk together the remaining 2 tablespoons of sugar, all-purpose flour, salt, and baking powder. Add the flour mixture to the butter and sugar, beating until properly combined. Stir in the water until the mixture begins to crumble. Fold in the chopped pecans. Crumble and strew the mixture over the filling in the casserole dish.

4. In a small glass bowl, whisk together the buttermilk and egg yolk. Carefully drizzle the egg mixture over everything in the casserole dish.

5. Place the dish in the oven, and bake for 35-40 minutes, or until the crumble topping is nicely toasted.

6. Serve the cobbler warm with a topping of your choice, such as vanilla ice cream or whipped cream.

Per Serving:
Calories: 287; Total fat: 8g; Saturated Fat: 3g; Carbohydrates: 53g; Protein: 4g; Sodium: 152 mg; Fiber: 3g

FIGGY CHEESE PISTACHIO TRUFFLES

COOK TIME: 0 MINS | MAKES: 6 SERVINGS

INGREDIENTS:

- 1/2 cup dried figs, finely chopped
- 1/2 cup pistachios, shells removed, finely chopped
- 1/4 cup plain cream cheese
- 4 oz. soft fresh goat cheese
- 1/3 tsp. freshly ground black pepper
- 1/8 tsp. kosher salt
- 1/8 tsp. ground nutmeg
- 1/8 tsp. ground cinnamon
- 2 tsp. freshly squeezed lemon juice
- Wild raw honey for drizzling

DIRECTIONS:

1. Mix together the figs and pistachios on a clean baking sheet.

2. Use a stand mixer to beat the cream cheese and goat cheese for a few minutes, until properly combined and lump-free. Stir in the pepper, salt, nutmeg, cinnamon, and lemon juice.

3. Form the mixture into small balls of roughly the same size, and roll them in the pistachios and figs before placing them on a serving platter. Use a fork to lightly drizzle the truffles with wild honey. If the honey is too thick to drizzle, heat it in the microwave for 10 seconds.

4. Serve the truffles, and enjoy.

Per Serving:
Calories: 172; Total Fat: 12g; Carbohydrates: 11g; Protein: 7g; Sodium: 167 mg; Fiber 2g

DECADENT EGGLESS CHOCOLATE MOUSSE

COOK TIME: 5 MINS | MAKES: 4 SERVINGS

INGREDIENTS:

- 1 cup dark dairy milk chocolate, chopped
- 1/3 tsp. kosher salt
- 1/2 tsp. pure vanilla essence
- 2 tsp. full-cream milk
- 2 tbsp. dark brown sugar (divided)
- 1/2 cup aquafaba at room temperature
- 1/2 tsp. cream of tartar
- Lightly toasted walnuts, chopped

DIRECTIONS:

1. Place the chopped chocolate in a glass bowl over a pot of boiling water. The water should not be touching the bottom of the bowl. Gently stir the chocolate as it melts. When the chocolate is completely smooth, transfer the bowl to a wooden chopping board.

2. Add the salt, vanilla, milk, and half of the sugar to the melted chocolate, stirring to combine.

3. Place the aquafaba in the large bowl of a stand mixer, and beat on high for about 1 minute, until light and bubbly. Gently beat in the cream of tartar, until the mixture resembles a cloud. Beat in the remaining sugar, until the cloud forms stiff peaks.

4. Working in about 3 or 4 batches, add the fluffy aquafaba to the melted chocolate, and use an offset spatula to gently fold the ingredients together. You want to be as gentle as possible.

5. Once all of the aquafaba has been folded into the melted chocolate, scoop the mixture into 4 glass bowls. Refrigerate covered for a few hours.

6. When the mousse is properly chilled, sprinkle with the walnuts, and serve.

Per Serving:
Calories: 240; Total Fat: 13g; Carbohydrates: 36g; Protein: 2g; Sodium: 45 mg; Fiber: 3g

CRISPY PISTACHIO BISCOTTI COOKIES

COOK TIME: 1 HOUR | MAKES: 12 SERVINGS

INGREDIENTS:

- 1 tbsp. finely grated lemon zest
- 1/4 tsp. kosher salt
- 1/2 tsp. ground nutmeg
- 1/2 tsp. ground cinnamon
- 1/2 tsp. baking soda
- 1/2 cup packed flax meal
- 2 cups almond flour
- 1 tsp. freshly squeezed lemon juice
- 1 tbsp. pure almond essence
- 2 tbsp. sunflower oil
- 1/2 tsp. pure vanilla essence
- 2 large free-range eggs
- Low-carb sweetener to taste (optional)
- 1/3 cup unsalted pistachio nuts, shells removed

DIRECTIONS:

1. Set the oven to preheat to 285°F, with the wire rack in the center of the oven. Cover a large baking tray with greaseproof paper.

2. In a large mixing bowl, whisk together the lemon zest, salt, nutmeg, cinnamon, baking soda, flax meal, and almond flour. Use a wooden spoon to stir in the lemon juice, almond essence, sunflower oil, vanilla essence, eggs, optional sweetener, and pistachio nuts, until the dough just comes together.

3. Use your hands to gather the dough together in a smooth ball. Form the dough into a large log that fits the length of your prepared baking tray. Bake in the oven for about 45 minutes. Remove the log from the oven, and cool on the counter for 15-20 minutes before using a very sharp knife to slice it into 12 equal slices.

4. Lower the oven temperature to 250°F. Lay the slices out on the same baking tray, and return the tray to the oven for a final 40 minutes. Use a spatula to gently flip the cookies halfway through the baking time.

5. Remove the tray from the oven, and let the cookies cool for an hour or two before eating.

Tip: The cookies can be stored in the cupboard in an airtight container for no more than 2 weeks.

Per Serving:
Calories: 207; Total Fat: 17.7 g; Saturated Fat: 1.9g; Carbohydrates: 7.1g; Protein: 7.2 g; Fiber: 4.2 g

ZINGY LOW-CARB LEMON CAKE

COOK TIME: 35-40 MINS | MAKES: 6-8 SERVINGS

INGREDIENTS:

- Whites of 6 large eggs
- Yolks of 6 large eggs
- Fine zest of 2 lemons
- 1 tbsp. freshly squeezed lemon juice
- 1/3 cup coconut oil, melted
- 1 tbsp. pure vanilla essence
- Low-carb sweetener to taste (optional)
- 1 tsp. bicarbonate of soda

- 1/4 cup collagen powder
- 1/2 cup coconut flour
- 2 cups almond flour
- 1/2 cup large unsweetened coconut flakes
- 1/4 cup low-fat cream cheese
- 1 cup heavy whipping cream
- 1/2 tsp. vanilla powder

DIRECTIONS:

1. Set the oven to preheat to 285°F, with the wire rack in the center of the oven. Cover a large, rimmed baking pan with greaseproof paper.

2. Whisk the egg whites using a handheld mixer, until stiff peaks form. In a separate bowl, whisk together the egg yolks, lemon zest, lemon juice, melted coconut oil, and vanilla essence. Use a third separate bowl to whisk together the optional low-carb sweetener, bicarbonate of soda, collagen powder, coconut flour, and almond flour.

3. Beat the flour mixture into the bowl of the egg yolk mixture, until you have a lump-free batter. Use an offset spatula to very gently fold the stiff egg whites into the batter. Don't ever mix.

4. Scrape the batter into the prepared baking pan in an even layer. Place the pan in the oven, and bake until the center is firm, and the top is nicely browned – about 35-40 minutes. Allow the cake to cool completely before adding the top layer.

5. While the cake cools, set the oven to preheat to 350°F, with the wire rack in the upper third of the oven. Fan the coconut flakes out in an even layer on a dry baking sheet. Bake in the oven for 2-3 minutes, until the flakes are nicely toasted. Set the sheet aside on the counter to cool.

6. In a large bowl, whisk together the cream cheese, heavy whipping cream, and vanilla powder, until the topping is light and fluffy with stiff peaks.

7. Spread the topping over the cooled cake, and garnish with the toasted coconut flakes before serving.

Tip: Coconut flakes tend to soften when refrigerated. If you are planning to store the cake, and would like to keep the flakes crispy, only add the flakes on each slice right before serving. The cake can be stored in the fridge for up to 5 days in an airtight container, or frozen for no more than 3 months.

Per Serving: Calories: 432; Total Fat: 38.6; Saturated Fat: 17.8g; Carbohydrates: 8.3g; Protein: 13.6g; Fiber: 4.1g

ALMOND CRUSTED RASPBERRY TART

COOK TIME: 12-15 MINS | MAKES: 6 SERVINGS

INGREDIENTS:

- 1/8 tsp. kosher salt
- 1/4 tsp. ground cinnamon
- 1/4 tsp. ground nutmeg
- 1 tbsp. raw honey
- 3 tbsp. unsalted butter, melted
- 1 1/4 cups almond flour
- 1/4 cup dark dairy milk chocolate, chopped
- 8 oz. cream cheese at room temperature
- 2 tbsp. amaretto liqueur
- 1 1/2 cups fresh raspberries

DIRECTIONS:

1. Set the oven to preheat to 350°F, with the wire rack in the center of the oven. Lightly coat a large pie pan with baking spray.

2. In a large mixing bowl, whisk together the salt, cinnamon, nutmeg, honey, butter, and almond flour. Use your hands to bring the dough together. Firmly press the dough into the prepared pie pan, and bake in the oven for 12-15 minutes, or until nicely browned. The edges should just about be lifting away from the sides of the pan. Allow the crust to cool completely in the pan.

3. When the crust is completely cool, remove from the pan, and place on a serving platter. Place the chocolate in a small glass bowl, and microwave on high for 1 1/2 minutes, stirring every 30 seconds. Brush the melted chocolate over the bottom of the crust, and halfway up the sides of the border.

4. Place the cream cheese in a large bowl. Use a hand mixer to beat the cheese for 1 minute, until smooth and lump-free. Gently beat in the amaretto liqueur.

5. Scrape the filling into the prepared pie crust, and garnish with the fresh raspberries before serving.

Per Serving:
Calories: 405; Total Fat: 34g; Carbohydrates: 19g; Protein: 8g; Sodium: 70g; Fiber: 4g

DARK CHOCOLATE HAZELNUT TRUFFLES

COOK TIME: 40-55 MINS | MAKES: 12 SERVINGS

INGREDIENTS:

- 1 3/4 cups blanched hazelnuts (divided)
- low-carb sweetener to taste (optional)
- 1 tsp. ground cinnamon
- 1/4 tsp. ground nutmeg
- 1/4 cup cocoa powder
- 1/4 cup collagen powder
- 4 tbsp. unsalted butter
- 1/2 cup coconut butter
- 1 oz. cocoa butter
- 2 1/2 oz. dark dairy milk chocolate, chopped

DIRECTIONS:

1. Set the oven to preheat to 285°F, with the wire rack in the center of the oven. Cover a large baking tray with greaseproof paper.

2. Fan the hazelnuts out over a clean baking tray. Dry roast the nuts in the oven for 40-50 minutes, until nicely toasted. Cool on the counter while you prepare the rest of the dish.

3. Transfer 1 cup of the roasted hazelnuts to a blender, and pulse a few times. You want an almost fine, chunky mixture. Add the optional sweetener, cinnamon, nutmeg, cocoa, collagen, unsalted butter, and coconut butter to the blender, and pulse until the ingredients come together to form a dough. Gather the dough into a smooth ball, and cover in cling wrap before chilling for 1 hour.

4. Remove 12 hazelnuts from the pan, and set aside. Crumble the rest of the nuts into a large mixing bowl.

5. Place the cocoa butter and dark chocolate in a glass bowl. Microwave on high for about 1 1/2 minutes, stirring every 30 seconds until the chocolate is completely melted.

6. Once the dough is nicely chilled, form the mixture into 12 truffles of roughly the same size. Press one of the reserved hazelnuts into the center of each truffle. Cover the hazelnuts in the center of each truffle, and smooth out the surface. Place the 12 truffles on the prepared baking tray, and place the tray in the freezer for 15 minutes.

7. Gently spear each chilled truffle with a toothpick. Hold each truffle over the bowl of melted chocolate, and spoon the mixture over the ball while turning the toothpick to coat the ball. The chocolate will harden quickly, so immediately roll the coated truffle in the chopped hazelnuts. Return the coated truffle to the pan. Repeat the process with the remaining truffles. Drizzle any remaining chocolate and nuts over all of the truffles. Serve and enjoy.

Tip: The truffles can be kept in the fridge for up to 3 days, or frozen for no more than 3 months. Don't over-chill the truffles, as this will cause the chocolate to crack immediately when coating them.

Per Serving:
Calories: 283; Total Fat: 27.9g; Saturated Fat: 13.1g; Carbohydrates: 7.4g; Protein: 6.6g; Fiber: 4.5g

CHEESE & MINT GRILLED WATERMELON

COOK TIME: 10-15 MINS | MAKES: 4 SERVINGS

INGREDIENTS:

- 1/4 cup balsamic vinegar
- 1 tsp. raw wild honey
- 1/8 tsp. ground nutmeg
- 4 thick watermelon slices, rind on
- 1 tbsp. sunflower oil
- 1/8 tsp. kosher salt
- 4 oz. soft chevre cheese
- 1/4 cup fresh mint leaves, roughly chopped

DIRECTIONS:

1. Set a grill to preheat to 400°F.

2. In a small pot over medium heat, bring the balsamic vinegar to a gentle simmer. Simmer uncovered while stirring, for about 4 minutes, or until the vinegar has evaporated by half. Transfer the pot to a wooden chopping board, and whisk in the honey and nutmeg until properly combined.

3. Use a basting brush to coat the watermelon slices with the sunflower oil, and lightly season each slice with the salt. Place the seasoned slices on the preheated grill. Grill the first side for 5 minutes, or just until the grill marks become apparent. Flip the watermelon, and grill the other side for an additional 3 minutes, or until the grill marks appear. Transfer the watermelons to a plate, and discard the rinds.

4. Place two slices of watermelon on a clean serving platter. Divide the cheese between the two slices, and spread it in an even layer over them. Place the second slice on top of the cheese. Drizzle the slices with the honey and balsamic vinegar, and garnish with the fresh mint. Serve immediately.

Per Serving:
Calories: 158; Total Fat: 10g; Carbohydrates: 12g; Protein: 6g; Sodium: 207g; Fiber: 1g

DECADENTLY SIMPLE CHOCOLATE PUDDING

COOK TIME: 15 MINS | MAKES: 4 SERVINGS

INGREDIENTS:

- 1/8 tsp. kosher salt
- 2 tbsp. pure cocoa powder
- 2 tbsp. dark brown sugar
- 3 tbsp. corn flour
- 2 cups almond milk
- 1 tsp. pure vanilla essence

DIRECTIONS:

1. In a small pot, whisk together the salt, cocoa powder, sugar, and corn flour. Whisk in the milk, and whisk the mixture over medium heat until the pudding begins to bubble. Once the pudding is bubbling, lower the heat to low, and gently whisk for an additional 2 minutes.

2. Transfer the pot to a wooden chopping board, and whisk in the vanilla. Leave the pot on the counter to cool, stirring at regular intervals to prevent a crust from forming. The cooling process should take about 15 minutes.

3. Scoop the pudding into serving bowls, and cover the bowls with cling wrap. Chill the pudding for a minimum of 30 minutes before serving.

Per Serving:
Calories: 127; Total Fat: 2g; Saturated Fat: 0g; Carbohydrates: 25g; Protein: 3g; Sodium: 112 mg; Fiber: 1g

NUTTY STUFFED FIGS

COOK TIME: 30 MINS | MAKES: 36 SERVINGS

INGREDIENTS:

- 36 dried Calimyrna figs
- 1/8 tsp. ground cloves
- 1/4 tsp. ground cinnamon
- 1/4 tsp. ground nutmeg
- 3 tbsp. pure cocoa powder
- 3 tbsp. raw honey (divided)
- 2/3 cup lightly toasted walnuts, chopped
- 2/3 cup lightly toasted pecans, chopped
- 4 1/2 tsp. freshly squeezed lemon juice
- 1/2 cup pomegranate juice

DIRECTIONS:

1. Set the oven to preheat to 350°F, with the wire rack in the center of the oven. Lightly coat a large baking dish with cooking spray.

2. Discard the fig stems, and slice an x over the stem hole, two-thirds of the way down each fig.

3. In a small glass bowl, stir together the cloves, cinnamon, nutmeg, cocoa powder, 1 tablespoon of honey, walnuts, and pecans. Gently stuff about 1 teaspoon of the mixture into each fig. Arrange the stuffed figs in the prepared baking dish.

4. In a separate clean glass bowl, whisk together the remaining honey, lemon juice, and pomegranate juice. Carefully spoon the mixture over all of the figs in the baking dish.

5. Cover the dish with tin foil, and bake in the oven for 20 minutes, basting the figs with the juices from the pan every 5 minutes. After 20 minutes, discard the foil, and return the dish to the oven for an additional 8-10 minutes, or until the figs are fork-tender. Continue basting every few minutes to prevent the figs from drying out.

6. Allow the figs to cool for a few minutes before serving.

Per Serving:
Calories: 98; Total Fat: 3g; Saturated Fat: 0g; Carbohydrates: 17g; Protein: 1g; Sodium: 3 mg; Fiber: 3g

Made in the USA
Middletown, DE
05 June 2022

66713419R00080